A TRAVELER'S GUIDE TO

116

WESTERN GREAT LAKES

Lighthouses

Text: Laurie Penrose
Maps: Bill T. Penrose
Photos: Ruth and Bill J. Penrose

Friede Publications

A Traveler's Guide to 116 Western Great Lakes Lighthouses
Copyright, 1995, by Laurie Penrose and Bill Penrose

COVER DESIGN: Boyer Pennington Studios, Inc.

Friede Publications
2339 Venezia Drive
Davison, Michigan 48423

Printed in the United States of America

First Printing, May 1995

OTHER GUIDEBOOKS BY FRIEDE PUBLICATIONS

A Traveler's Guide to 100 Eastern Great Lakes Lighthouses

A Traveler's Guide to 116 Michigan Lighthouses

A Guide to 199 Michigan Waterfalls

Natural Michigan

Michigan State and National Parks: A Complete Guide

Ultimate Michigan Adventures

Canoeing Michigan Rivers

Fish Michigan — 100 Southern Michigan Lakes

Fish Michigan — 100 Northern Lower Michigan Lakes

Fish Michigan — 100 Upper Peninsula Lakes

Fish Michigan — 50 Rivers

CONTENTS

GREEN BAY INSET

ONTARIO

Thunder Bay

MINNESOTA

LAKE SUPERIOR

Duluth

MICHIGAN

Sault Ste. Marie

Georgian Bay

LAKE HURON

WISCONSIN

Green Bay
(See Inset)

LAKE MICHIGAN

Milwaukee

MICHIGAN

ONTARIO

Chicago

LAKE ERIE

ILLINOIS

INDIANA

OHIO

ACKNOWLEDGMENTS

Once again we would like to express our sincere gratitude to the many people who have helped us with our family project. As we traveled the Great Lakes, we found the people near their shores to be very proud of their maritime heritage and very informed about the history of the lakes. It is to these friendly people — the people of the lakes — that we would like to say, "Thank You!"

And a special thanks goes to the following groups and individuals.

<u>IN CANADA</u>:

Judy Beth Armstrong, *Assistant Library Director*, and Pat Frook, *Administrative Assistant*, Owen Sound (Ontario) Public Library

Monique Benoit, Government Archives Division, and Gilles Marengere, Circulation desk, National Archives of Canada, Ottawa, Ontario

Marie Cruickshank, Collingwood, Ontario, whose grandfather helped build lighthouses in Ontario

George Dodds, Manitowaning, Ontario

Terry and Kay Gaffney for inviting us to their family outing at the Strawberry Island lighthouse. It was the perfect afternoon.

David Green, Pointe Au Baril, Ontario, for the snowmobile trip to Pt. Au Baril lighthouse

Captain Jerry Marcil, wife Sharon and son Jason, Britt, Ontario

Captain Hiram Monague, Christian Island, Ontario

Isobel and Nick Pipoli, Batchawana Bay, Ontario

Laurine Tremaine, Local History Collections, Parry Sound Public Library

Greg and Lynda Richard, Rossport Island Tours, Thunder Bay Ontario

Nancy Rouble, Sault Ste. Marie (Ontario) Public Library

Margaret White, Friends of the Library, Meaford, Ontario

We would also like to express our sincere appreciation to the many men and women of the Canadian Coast Guard who have been of so much help. We would especially like to thank Mr. Allan McNeice, Canadian Coast Guard, Thunder Bay, Ontario; Mr. Albert (Bert) Saasto, Canadian Coast Guard Retired, Assistant Keeper Battle Island Lightstation, Ontario; Mr. Mark Senecal, Canadian Coast Guard Ship *Caribou Isle*; and Mr. Ron Walker, Canadian Coast Guard Station, Parry Sound, Ontario.

FRONT COVER PHOTO: Old Michigan City Lighthouse Museum, page 1.

IN THE UNITED STATES:

Marsha Boyd, *Library Director*, and Amy Winter and Kathy Zettel, *Assistant Librarians*, West Branch Public Library, West Branch, Michigan

Chicago Historical Society, Chicago, Illinois

Rose and Louie Janda, *Caretakers*, Cana Island Lighthouse, Wisconsin

Kenosha Historical Society, Kenosha, Wisconsin

The *Kenosha News* Library, Kenosha, Wisconsin

Linda N. Nenn, Light Station Restoration Committee of Port Washington, Wisconsin

David Snyder, *Park Historian*, Apostle Islands National Lakeshore, Bayfield, Wisconsin

Dave Strzok, Brad Marcouiller, Lisa Gurnoe, Denise Carlson and Dave Thoen, Apostle Islands Cruise Service, Bayfield, Wisconsin

Tim Sweet, Friends of Rock Island, Clintonville, Wisconsin

Yolande Wersching, Cudahy Library, Loyala University, Chicago, Illinois

And another sincere thank you to the many men and women of the United States Coast Guard who have helped us so often. A special thank you to BM2 Philip Myer, Calumet Harbor Coast Guard Station, Chicago, Illinois.

GREAT LAKES LIGHTHOUSE KEEPERS ASSOCIATION

The Great Lakes Lighthouse Keepers Association is a nonprofit organization "dedicated to the preservation of the lighthouses and the history of the people who kept them."

They offer valuable assistance to local groups trying to save lighthouses, and their own preservation work on the St. Helena Island Lighthouse, near the Straits of Mackinac, has earned the organization national recognition.

By including youth groups in their work, the association is also accomplishing their goal of "developing a new generation of preservationists" who will be ready to take on their own projects.

You can contact the Great Lakes Lighthouse Keepers Association at P.O. Box 580, Allen Park, MI 48101.

Members receive The Beacon, a quarterly newsletter that includes information about ongoing projects around the lakes, plus firsthand historical accounts of what life was like at the lakes' lighthouses.

PREFACE

Walking to a lighthouse at the end of a pier or a breakwater can be very pleasant and relaxing during good weather. But when waves wash over these structures, especially during high winds and storms, they become extremely dangerous. Footing is precarious, especially for children. So please use good judgment and caution when visiting those lights. During threatening weather, stay off breakwaters.

COURTESY

Some lighthouses are on private property and are even used as private residences. We urge you to be considerate and respect the rights of their owners. View them from a distance on public land or from the water, and when that is not possible, simply do not attempt to visit at all.

One of my earliest memories of the Great Lakes is being at a picnic with my family at Presque Isle Park in Marquette, Michigan. After a day of exploring the wooded paths and rocky shoreline that nearly surrounded the park, my brother, sister and myself, plus an assortment of cousins, were sent down to the lake to refill our empty pop bottles, exchanging syrupy sweetness for the refreshing purity of Lake Superior.

When we began researching *A Traveler's Guide to 116 Michigan Lighthouses*, I was able to revisit Presque Isle Park and many other nearly forgotten places from my childhood, and I once again felt the magnetic pull of the Great Lakes. Not long after publication of that guidebook, our family decided to expand our horizons by writing about lighthouses throughout all the Great Lakes. We were somewhat apprehensive, since it wasn't officially our "home territory," and in fact it turned out to be a much larger project than we had anticipated.

But the results were well worth the effort. My wife Ruth and I have met many, many people in both the United States and Canada who share our interest in and love for the Great Lakes.

And our research travels compressed a lifetime worth of outstanding experiences and fond memories into just a few years. We have spent summer days at peaceful Canal Park in Duluth, Minnesota, watching the ships glide past as they approached the lift bridge there. We have hiked along sandy Minnesota Point, and its sister to the south, Wisconsin Point, and on each visit come upon black bears that had decided to enjoy the seclusion of the point before we had. We were fortunate to have attended a First Nations Pow-Wow on majestic and powerful Mt. McKay in Thunder Bay, Ontario. As our travels extended eastward, we took a beautiful sunset cruise on the St. Lawrence River with Captain Bernie Coffey, who guided us to the picturesque Sisters Island lighthouse. In between, the mighty Soo Locks and Welland Canal fueled the imagination, and I never stopped thinking of how fortunate we are to have seen so much of these beautiful Great Lakes.

But two trips stand out in my mind as favorites. One was to Rossport, Ontario, where we visited Battle Island lightstation with Albert Saasto, the last lightkeeper on the Great Lakes. Hearing his firsthand accounts of living on the island was a thrill; nothing can compare to such oral histories for bringing alive the Great Lakes. The other was a one-week working vacation Ruth and I took with our daughter Laurie and her children, Masina, 5, and Alex, 3. We rode the train from Sarnia, Ontario, to Ottawa to visit the Canadian National Archives to gather information on Canadian lights. The highlight of the trip for Ruth and me was seeing our grandchildren board the train and visiting the archives with us. We hope that we have had a part in planting the seed for — as the Great Lakes Lighthouse Keepers' motto says — "A New Generation of Preservationists."

We all have our own part to play, and that lesson was brought home to me several years ago, when we first began writing about lighthouses. During a

Memorial Day weekend visit to South Manitou Island in Lake Michigan, I noticed the undecorated grave of a young American veteran who, as his ultimate act of patriotism, had given his life in Archangel, Russia. In my mind's eye, I contrasted the bright flags honoring the graves on the mainland to that of this young man, lying long forgotten. I couldn't help wondering if we were somehow neglecting our past, as well as our future, which had become evident in the neglected remains of a few lighthouses I had recently visited.

The brief cemetery visit was half forgotten when a year later I left Grand Portage, Minnesota, on a lighthouse cruise to Isle Royale National Park. On board I met another lighthouse enthusiast, David McCormick from Northport, Michigan. After talking awhile, he told me of his trips during the boating season to decorate a veteran's grave on South Fox Island.

I was brought up short. While I had stood in a shaded cemetery only shaking my head over a forgotten veteran, McCormick had acted on his convictions. It was then I realized that we each have a part to play, and an obligation to act, but it is only through following our hearts and dreams that we can become aware of of what our part is.

As Ruth and I approach retirement age, we thank God for the opportunities we have had, and we plan to continue traveling the Great Lakes as much as possible. Our family's most important goal has been to bring the Great Lakes wonders to you, and we sincerely hope that you enjoy them. Once you feel the magic of the Great Lakes, it will be with you always.

If I had a chance to live my life again, all I would ask is that I could relive it somewhere on the Great Lakes.

Bill Penrose
WEST BRANCH, MICHIGAN

A new generation of lighthouse preservationists, Masina and Alex Rose.

Old Michigan City Lighthouse Museum

The Old Michigan City lighthouse is a beautiful two-story structure nestled on a snug rise looking over picturesque Trail Creek. The first story of the lighthouse is constructed of honey-colored brick, with a border of lighter brick at the top and bottom. Basement windows are topped with a heavy lintel, while the tall first-floor windows are bordered by beautiful hunter-green trim, including an arch over each. The front windows are framed with even wider, more-intricate wood trim. A few steps lead up to the inviting entryway that is sheltered beneath the sweeping curve of a second-story balcony. Four supporting pillars are painted cream-colored to match the wood railing curving along the balcony's edge. A beautiful arched doorway leads out from the second story, which is covered with dark-green wood shingles interrupted by several windows.

In the back of the house, another porch provides a shady resting spot, and that overhang is also supported by four cream-colored pillars. The roof shingles are dark red, and just above the roofline the octagonal light surveys its surroundings. The parapet is painted a pristine white, and the matching white lantern room is glazed with long, narrow panes and capped in green.

Built into the side of the hill, the house has a walkout basement on its south side, with six-paned windows recessed into the white stone foundation.

This lighthouse was built in 1858; however, a light guarded the shores of Michigan City as early as 1837. Also in 1858 the first government lightkeeper was appointed — Harriet Colfax, an amazing women who had arrived in Michigan City a few years before from Ogdensburg, New York. She assisted her brother at his newspaper, and when the new lighthouse was built, she lobbied for the position as keeper. Appointed by her cousin Schuyler Colfax, who would later become vice-president of the United States under Grant, she was to light the lamps of Michigan City for over 45 years.

She lived in the lighthouse with her lifelong companion Ann Hartwell, a local schoolteacher. Until 1904, Harriet was responsible for lighting both the lamp atop her residence and also a pier light that stood in the harbor for many years until blown down in a gale. The fierce storms that raced down the length of Lake Michigan often made it near impossible for Harriet to service the pier light, but she never failed in her duty, earning the respect and admiration of the hardened sailors who depended on her to guide them safely home.

In 1904 the keeper's home was remodeled and the beacon from its roof was moved out to the pier. It wasn't until 1963 that the keeper's house was sold by the Coast Guard to the town of Michigan City to be used for historical purposes.

Today, this beautiful dwelling houses the Old Lighthouse Museum. The surrounding lawn is dotted with large displays, from a white surf boat and heavy steel capstan to a towering wood rudder that serves as flagpole marking the front entrance of the home. Inside, exhibits of the period — including an ornate pot-bellied stove and decorative tin ceiling — fuel the imagination.

The museum is open 1-4 p.m. Tuesday through Sunday year round. The

"The rich notes of the carousel's calliope drifted through the open windows during summer nights."

CLASSIC FRESNEL LENS ON DISPLAY IN OLD MICHIGAN CITY LIGHTHOUSE MUSEUM

OLD MICHIGAN CITY LIGHTHOUSE MUSEUM

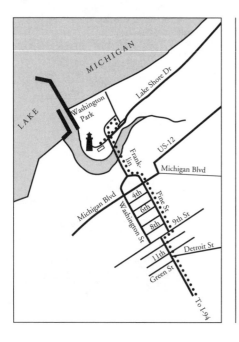

lighthouse complex is part of much larger Washington Park, a generous area of land that includes the Coast Guard Station, a zoo, a marina, and a beach. During the 1930s, families living at the lighthouse made good use of the park, attending dances and concerts, and the rich notes of the carousel's calliope drifted through the open windows during summer nights.

DIRECTIONS: From I-94 at Michigan City, exit onto US-421 (also called Franklin St.) and go north approximately 3.8 miles to 9th St. (which is one-way). Turn right (east) onto 9th and go one block to Pine St. (also one-way). Turn left (north) onto Pine and go about ½ mile — as it crosses US-12 (Michigan Blvd.), curves left, then right — to Franklin St. Follow Franklin about 0.3 mile over a bridge and into Washington Park. As you cross the bridge, look for the lighthouse, to the left on Lake Shore Dr. However, you cannot turn left onto Lake Shore, but rather must bear right about a block and, staying in the left lane, make a U-turn at the turn around and then go west on Lake Shore Dr. one block past Franklin St.

Michigan City East Pierhead Light

Michigan City lies at the eastern edge of the Indiana Dunes, an area filled with rugged tree-covered mounds that sweep back from the shore in waves. Michigan City's East Pier extends north from a small beach out into Lake Michigan, then angles abruptly to the west. The surface of the cement pier is beginning to crumble, and the beautiful catwalk — a row of pillars, each branching out at the top to support the platform — shows neglect in its rusty exterior.

That will change, though, if the people of Michigan City are successful in their refurbishing efforts. Although much of the catwalk was destroyed by the infamous November 1913 storm, it was later rebuilt and has won a place in the hearts of local residents. In 1983, concerned citizens fought a Coast Guard decision to raze the catwalk. The townspeople won, and the following year both the light and the catwalk were placed on the National Register of Historic Places. In 1991 the Coast Guard donated the catwalk to the city of Michigan City, and its fate is now more secure.

The catwalk extends to the end of the pier, where the large light has guarded the entrance to Trail Creek since 1904. Built on a square concrete foundation that rises above the pier, the walls of the 50-foot-tall, white steel structure are streaked with rust and marred with graffiti. Above the second story, the catwalk entrance extends from the steeply sloped red roof, which adds a bit of color. The white, octagonal light tower extends 20 feet above the roofline, and a black steel walkway surrounds the black lantern room, which is glazed in triangular panes.

Across a channel to the northwest, an outer breakwater light, built in 1911, sits on a narrow strip of dark stone that is beginning to crumble away in large portions. The white, 30-foot-high tower has a small, red beacon on top and a red triangle prominently displayed on the side.

The west bank of the river is defined by a small pier that extends into Lake Michigan. At its end a white skeletal tower with red beacon and triangle assists mariners in their approach to the rivermouth. Near the pier a nuclear plant's tower, with its telltale curve, sits close to the water, while in the distance the shore is lined with the pale sands of the Indiana Dunes, with bands of deep green stretching down to touch Lake Michigan.

"Although much of the cat-walk was destroyed by the infamous November 1913 storm, it was later rebuilt and has won a place in the hearts of local residents."

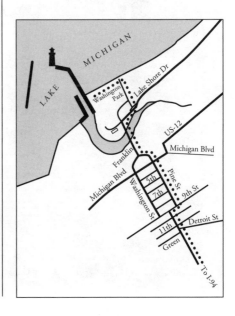

⚓ DIRECTIONS: From I-94 at Michigan City, exit onto US-421 (also called Franklin St.) and go north approximately 3.8 miles to 9th St. (which is one-way). Turn right (east) onto 9th and go one block to Pine St. (also one-way). Turn left (north) onto Pine and go about ½ mile — as it crosses US-12 (Michigan Blvd.), curves left, then right — to Franklin St. Follow Franklin about 0.3 mile over a bridge to Lake Shore Dr. in Washington Park. Turn right (east) onto Lake Shore and go about 0.1 mile to a street (the first reached) that leads left (north) to the beach and zoo parking area. Drive to the west end of the parking area for the shortest walk to the pierhead light. You can also make a much farther walk from the Old Michigan City Lighthouse Museum area.

MICHIGAN CITY EAST PIERHEAD LIGHT

Gary Breakwater Light

The Gary Breakwater light is a 30-foot-tall, round, red metal tower guarding the city of Gary's harbor. The wide base narrows slightly as it rises to support a round walkway and lantern room. The cross-hatched panes of the lantern room give the light a vintage flair, contrasting with the more-recent addition of a ladder that reaches to the very top of the structure, where a modern green beacon has been added.

This light rests at the end of a private industrial pier and can only be viewed from the water.

" The cross-hatched panes of the lantern room give the light a vintage flair. "

Buffington Harbor Breakwater Light

The Buffington Harbor Breakwater light rests atop a circle of smooth concrete at the end of a very rough breakwater. Jumbled piles of huge stone blocks stretch to encircle the light's platform and then gradually submerge themselves in the murky, green depths of Lake Michigan.

The first level of the faded red tower is an oval with a flat-roofed room on one end and the narrow tower rising from the other. Its smooth sides are interrupted by only a few small round windows, while above, a round parapet protects the octagonal lantern room.

This light is on a privately maintained industrial pier and can only be viewed from the water.

Indiana Harbor East Breakwater Light

The Indiana Harbor light sits at the end of a half-mile-long pier stretching into the deep green of Lake Michigan. The tower rests atop an unusual foundation of huge, loosely fitted square blocks encircled with a band of metal sheathing for reinforcement. The pier is also constructed in the same manner, but unfortunately was not reinforced with metal. As a result, many of the large blocks of stone have tumbled into the water, creating a very rough pier. A metal catwalk extends from shore, ending at a square platform that surrounds the tower. Wide arches on each side of the concrete platform form four heavy legs that rest on as many green pedestals, similar to the Port Washington, Wisconsin, light. The platform is secured with a green metal railing, and a small door opens to the interior of the light.

The square, white metal tower has only a few round windows on its first story. Above, the tower tapers abruptly, while a round window protrudes from each side of the building. The slender tower rises nearly 60 feet, and at its summit a modern beacon protects the harbor waters.

This light is on an industrial pier, which is privately maintained. It can only be viewed from the water.

"The tower rests atop an unusual foundation of huge, loosely fitted square blocks."

Calumet Harbor Lighthouse

"The pier is so long that the lighthouse is technically in Indiana."

In 1853, the small but thriving town of Calumet was designated to receive a light that was to assist vessels approaching Chicago, 13 miles to the north. Once installed, however, the new light was frequently mistaken *as* Chicago's, which led to Calumet's beacon being shut down. But by 1873, because of the incredible growth of Calumet as a major harbor, the area received another light. In 1875 a pier light replaced that shore light. A year later the better lens of the old shore light was removed and installed in the new pier light.

Along with economic growth, Calumet must have had its share of social ills. Not long after a lifesaving service was established on the lighthouse property in 1886, the personnel stationed here requested permission to surround their yard with a fence as protection from teenage gangs that roamed the area.

The pier light was moved in 1884 and rebuilt in 1898. It served as Calumet's main light until 1904, when the present lighthouse was built on a new, 7,000-foot-long breakwater. In recent years this enormous breakwater has caused problems for those wanting to add the lighthouse to Illinois structures on the National Register of Historic Places. The pier is so long that the lighthouse is technically in Indiana.

The breakwater is dominated by the light structure, which rests on a large, rectangular concrete foundation with a graceful curve of the wall facing the pier. Above the foundation is a white metal one-story building whose windows are now boarded up. The light tower rises from a corner of the flat roof and extends upward about 25 feet. Its round, white lantern room is surrounded by a black parapet and railing and is covered with a black metal roof. The crosshatched panes of the lantern provide one of the few artistic details in the spartan architecture of this light.

You can view the light from Calumet Park, which is filled with towering hardwoods and lush lawns. In front of the parking area, a small hill drops down toward the water's edge, where a walkway runs along the shore. Amenities include a beach and boat launch.

Calumet Harbor Breakwater South End Light

The Calumet Breakwater light is a skeletal steel tower supported by four small, yellow cylinders. The top half of the 35-foot-tall, square light is enclosed in metal siding, with the small modern beacon protruding from the roof. A black railing borders the roof's edge, while a tall, white radio antenna extends skyward.

The pier is constructed of large stone blocks loosely fitted into circular shapes and edged in heavy metal siding. These adjoining circles form an interesting outline for the pier as it stretches into the deep green of Lake Michigan.

" The adjoining circles form an interesting outline."

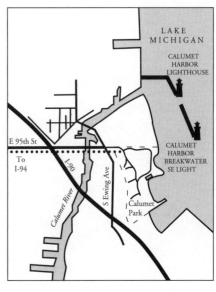

DIRECTIONS: To facilitate travel in the Chicago area, we recommend that you use a detailed Chicago-area map.

From I-94 north of Calumet City, take exit 65 (Stony Island) and follow the exit for approximately 1.5 miles to its end at 95th Street. Turn right (east) onto 95th and go approximately 2.5 miles to its end at Calumet Park. (Just before entering the park you will cross S. Ewing Ave.) In the park, you can follow the loop road in either direction. We went to the right, then just past the Field House turned to the left, past the Coast Guard Station to the parking area. The Calumet Harbor lighthouse is on the pierhead just north of the park, and the breakwater light is out in the harbor to the right.

Chicago Harbor Lighthouse

Chicago's first light was built in 1831 on the south bank of the Chicago River. On the day it was inspected and visited by dozens of people, the tower collapsed. The builder blamed a layer of quicksand deep below, while the public blamed the inferior materials used by the builder. Whatever the cause of the disaster, a new lighthouse was built the following year.

By 1847 the fast-growing port of Chicago called out for more guiding beacons, and so the first of several pier lights was built. In 1859 it was replaced by a new metal-skeleton tower, but it was only 11 years before the city's massive growth threatened it. In 1870, because of a barrier of thick smoke from local industries and the hundreds of steamships calling on Chicago, the light from the pier could hardly be seen. It was determined that a new light should be built in a more useful location, and so a lighthouse was established in Grossepoint, 13 miles away, and Chicago's pier light was darkened.

The lighthouse now standing on the breakwater was built in 1893 and originally stood on the end of North Pier, replacing the 1859 light, which was removed and sent to Wisconsin's Rawley Point. Earlier in 1893 the Lighthouse Service had showed off some of their innovations at a special outdoor exhibit at the Columbian Exhibition in Chicago. A tall metal tower was fitted with a third-order Fresnel lens, and a crew was assigned to light and extinguish it daily. When the fair ended, the tower was sent to Point Loma, California, and the beautiful Fresnel lens was installed in the newly completed North Pier lighthouse. In 1917 the breakwater was built, and the 24-year-old lighthouse was moved out to it.

Today, the best way to view that lighthouse is from the large Navy Pier, where large buildings rise up alongside luxury yachts offering dinner cruises of Chicago's harbor.

The Chicago Harbor lighthouse rests on a 12-foot-high cement foundation at the southern tip of the mile-long breakwater. A single-story cement building nearly fills the area atop the foundation, with just enough room surrounding to provide a small walkway enclosed with a metal railing. This building — really two separate buildings added when the tower was moved to the breakwater — houses a fog horn on one side of the light tower and a boathouse on the opposite. A dark-red roof covers the building, and the light tower — marked with an offset pattern of narrow, rectangular windows — rises 30 feet above the roofline. A walkway with black metal railing surrounds a small circular room that supports the lantern room, capped with black metal. The tower houses a working third-order Fresnel lens, which the Coast Guard still maintains despite this light sometimes being leased by a private individual.

The beauty of this lighthouse relies on its unique design. Because the tower was constructed first and was later embraced by the curving edges of the red roof and buildings, the tower walls are flush with the walls of the buildings. Entry is by way of a door — protected by a small, red overhang — at the tower's base, which rests on the cement foundation.

Until the beacon was automated in 1978, the tower was home to three keepers at a time. Being in such an isolated spot, yet so close to millions of people was

sometimes uncomfortable for the keepers. For new arrivals the stress was amplified — the newest man was assigned the highest bedroom, a curving room offering a fine view of the harbor but also closest to the ear-splitting fog signal, which sounded every 20 seconds around the clock when fog threatened the harbor.

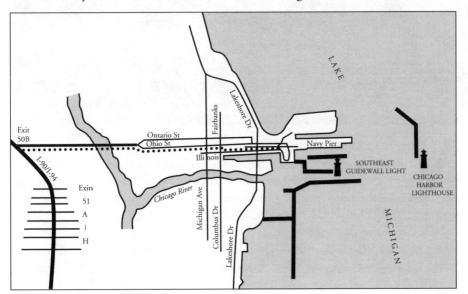

DIRECTIONS: To facilitate travel in Chicago, we recommend that you use a detailed city map.

From I-90/I-94 west of Chicago's downtown area, take exit 50-B and head east on the freeway spur into downtown Chicago. At approximately 0.8 mile the freeway ends on Ohio St., which is one way east. Follow Ohio approximately 0.8 mile to Fairbanks. Turn right (south) onto Fairbanks (which becomes Columbus Dr.) and go 2 blocks to Illinois St. Turn left (east) onto Illinois and go about 4 blocks, passing under Highway 41, to Navy Pier Park. Follow the park's loop road around to the right to the public parking areas.

You can walk out onto Navy Pier and view both the Harbor light, off the end of the pier to the southeast, and the Southeast Guidewall light, to the south.

To return to I-90/I-94 when leaving Navy Pier, continue around the loop, drive back under Highway 41, and go west on Ontario St. (which is one block north of Ohio St. and runs one way west) approximately one mile to the freeway entrance spur.

Chicago Harbor Southeast Guidewall Light

Not far south of Chicago's large, well-known Navy Pier is a smaller, unobtrusive pier with a smattering of young trees planted along its surface. To the north of that small pier, the remains of another, older pier rise just above the waterline, its huge pilings now worn and broken by the constant pounding of waves. Between the two, Chicago harbor's southeast guidewall stretches into the lake, and at its end stands a 30-foot-tall, white steel skeleton tower, built in 1938, that still aids sailors approaching the piers. The bottom half of the square tower is open, while the top portion is enclosed in steel siding and capped with a black parapet and lantern room.

DIRECTIONS and map, page 11.

Grossepoint Lighthouse Museum

The Grossepoint lighthouse was first lit in 1874 to assist in guiding ships into Chicago's harbor, 13 miles to the south. Its second-order Fresnel lens has an unusual history. During the Civil War, a lightkeeper in Florida was concerned that his light might fall into Confederate hands. So he took apart the Fresnel lens and buried it in the sand below the lighthouse. After the war it was excavated and returned to the U.S. Lighthouse Establishment in Washington D.C., just in time to be sent on to the new Grossepoint light.

The lighthouse is a beautiful ivory-colored 90-foot-tall tower whose original brick was surfaced with concrete in 1914 to counteract deterioration. The tower's smooth, tapered surface rises to a brick-red metal walkway with decorative supports of the same color beneath. Below those brackets, small arched windows — some bricked over — peer out in each direction. The walkway's delicate metal railing surrounds a circular room, which in turn supports a smaller walkway that

" He took apart the Fresnel lens and buried it in the sand below the lighthouse. "

" Twin whistle houses flank each side of the tower, an unusual detail that adds to the charm of this lightstation."

encircles the beautiful 12-sided lantern room, entirely glazed with square panes of glass and its second-order Fresnel lens still tucked inside. An assortment of pines and hardwoods have surrounded the base of the tower, stretching skyward to form a deep green contrast to the pale concrete.

Twin whistle houses flank each side of the tower, an unusual detail that adds to the charm of this lightstation. Narrow cement walks lead past lovely flower beds to duplicate entrances to the keeper's house, a feature necessitated by the fact that this dwelling was home to both the keeper and his assistant and their families. Covered in ivy, the house is cream-colored with brown trim, and each of the many windows is topped by a delicate arch.

In 1922 the light was converted to electricity and 13 years later was decommissioned and turned over to the city of Evanston. The tower was added to the original license agreement in 1941, and in 1946 the entire lightstation was turned over to the Evanston Historical Society for preservation.

The lighthouse is operated by the Lighthouse Park District of Evanston, which offers tours June through September on Saturdays and Sundays at 2, 3 and 4 p.m. A small admission fee is charged, and children under five years of age are not allowed. The facility is closed to the public from October through May.

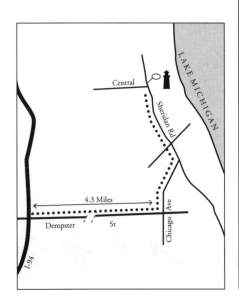

DIRECTIONS: From I-94 just north of Chicago, take exit #37 (Dempster St.) and follow Dempster east about 4.3 miles to Chicago Ave. Turn left (north) onto Chicago and go approximately 0.7 mile, curving left to a traffic signal. Continue straight, through the traffic signal, onto Sheridan Rd. and follow Sheridan about 0.9 mile to the traffic signal at Central St. Look for the lighthouse on the right, next to the Evanston Art Center. There is no parking area at the lighthouse, but parking is available on nearby streets within easy walking distance.

Waukegan Harbor Light

" A catwalk once stretched the length of the pier. "

The south pier at Waukegan, Illinois, stretches out into Lake Michigan nearly half a mile, and at its tip rests the round metal tower of the south pierhead light. At the base of the tower, a black metal stairway rises up a few feet to meet a narrow entry door. Near the top of the 25-foot-tall structure is a second entrance. A catwalk, now gone, once stretched the length of the pier to end at that doorway. A plain railing borders the tower's flat roof, and a modern beacon guides sailors approaching the harbor.

A lightstation was first built here in 1849, when the town was named Little Fort, but 11 years later that brick tower was torn down and a new beacon built atop the keeper's house. When the first pier light began shining in 1899, the shore light was extinguished but the structure was still utilized as a keeper's dwelling until 1908, when a new house was built closer to the pier. After another harbor light was added in 1905, the lightkeepers' quarters were moved to a more convenient residence.

DIRECTIONS: From I-94 west of Waukegan, take the Highway 132 (Grand Ave.) exit and go east about 6.1 miles on Grand, through Gurnee and to a traffic signal at Sheridan Rd. in Waukegan. Continue straight ahead, across Sheridan and over the Amstudz Freeway and railroad tracks, about 0.3 mile to Pershing Rd. (Although this last 0.3 mile is still Grand Ave., on some maps it is called Mathon Dr.) Turn right (south) onto Pershing and go approximately 0.2 mile to Madison St. Turn left (east) onto Madison St. and look for Government Pier one block to the right, near the boat launch area. Parking is available in this area. The light is located on the end of Government Pier.

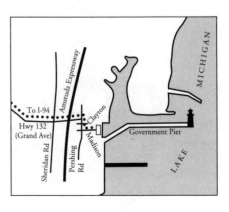

Kenosha
North Pier Light

The red steel tower of the Kenosha Pierhead light dominates the harbor and provides a beautiful silhouette against the backdrop of Lake Michigan. Situated at the end of a ribbed-steel-reinforced pier that helps form the north bank of a dredged canal into Kenosha's harbor, the round tower stretches up 45 feet to a black steel walkway and lantern room. An intricate top rail around the walkway blends well with the crosshatched panes of glass entirely surrounding the lantern room. An elongated ventilator shaft pokes out of top of the structure.

Along the shore north of the pier, a sandy beach lines the water's edge, separated from the parking area by a row of large boulders.

Another pier jutting from the south bank of the channel has a small steel cylinder light at its end, as does a breakwater directly out from the north pier. The light on the breakwater can be lined up with the north pier light to form a range to guide ships into the harbor.

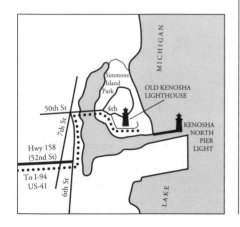

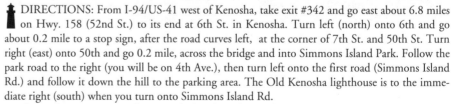 DIRECTIONS: From I-94/US-41 west of Kenosha, take exit #342 and go east about 6.8 miles on Hwy. 158 (52nd St.) to its end at 6th St. in Kenosha. Turn left (north) onto 6th and go about 0.2 mile to a stop sign, after the road curves left, at the corner of 7th St. and 50th St. Turn right (east) onto 50th and go 0.2 mile, across the bridge and into Simmons Island Park. Follow the park road to the right (you will be on 4th Ave.), then turn left onto the first road (Simmons Island Rd.) and follow it down the hill to the parking area. The Old Kenosha lighthouse is to the immediate right (south) when you turn onto Simmons Island Rd.

After parking, you can walk across the beach to the south to visit the North Pier light and also walk back up Simmons Island Rd. to see the Old Kenosha lighthouse.

An alternate route in is to stay on 4th Ave. past Simmons Island Rd. down the hill and to the left about 0.3 mile to its end at the beach area.

Kenosha Old Lighthouse

The old Southport lighthouse in Kenosha, built in 1866 on Simmons Island, stands next to Simmons Island Park, a lovely shoreline area that includes lush, shady lawns and a sandy beach with a fine view of the Kenosha Pier light.

The Old Southport light tower is a 60-foot-high conical structure constructed of light-brown brick randomly interrupted at various levels with a few small, square windows.

The tower, which became obsolete in 1906 when the North Pier light began guiding ships into the harbor, is now listed on the National Register of Historic Places and is being restored by the Kenosha County Historical Society. When we first visited in early 1994, the lantern room was missing, leaving a lonely space atop. Today, thanks to the heroic efforts of the historical society and the residents of Kenosha, the tower once again proudly displays a lantern room — a two-ton black metal replica of the original — which returns dignity to the town's proud landmark.

The tan brick keeper's dwelling near the tower is now a spacious private residence.

" The tower once again proudly displays a lantern room — a two-ton black metal replica of the original — which returns dignity to the town's proud landmark."

Racine North and South Breakwater Lights

" The North Breakwater light is known locally as 'Big Red.' "

The first light on Racine's north breakwater was erected in 1866. Two years later the pier was extended and a new light built near the end of the rugged stone wall. That 40-foot-high, red metal skeleton tower still guides mariners into Racine's harbor. Two flights of stairs lead to the upper half of the structure, which is enclosed in metal siding. Porthole windows illuminate the interior, while directly above, a square walkway surrounds the 10-sided lantern room. The tower, known locally as "Big Red," was slated to be demolished by the Coast Guard in 1987, but public protest saved the much-loved landmark.

The South Breakwater light is a white, 25-foot-tall steel skeleton tower with a square metal walkway and modern beacon on top. Sitting on its own stonepile breakwater, it too helps guide boats into Racine's inviting harbor and marina.

Beautiful Festival Park stretches out along the south breakwater, ending at an elevated platform that overlooks both lights and the waterfront of Racine.

RACINE NORTH BREAKWATER LIGHT

RACINE SOUTH BREAKWATER LIGHT

"Beautiful Festival Park stretches out along the south breakwater."

DIRECTIONS: If entering Racine from the south on Hwy. 32, follow Hwy. 32 north to the downtown area, where it goes right (east) on 7th St. about 5 blocks and then left (north) on Main St. From the intersection of 7th and Main, go north on Main 3 blocks to 4th St.

If you are entering Racine from the north on Hwy. 32, follow Hwy. 32 south 2 blocks past the junction with Hwy. 38 to 4th St.

Once at 4th St., turn east and go 3 blocks to the Racine on the Lake Festival Park. Continue straight ahead to the parking area at the far end of the park. You can view the lights from a platform just beyond the parking area. The North Breakwater light is across the harbor entrance, and the Old South Breakwater light is just in front of the viewing platform.

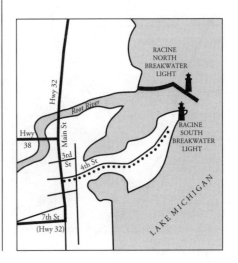

Wind Point Lighthouse

"Bordering the entire building is a wide cement walkway that, along with a few low-lying shrubs and young bushes planted nearby, gives the house a very crisp and organized profile."

FOGHORN BUILDING

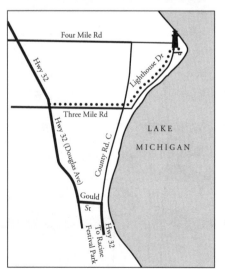

The Wind Point lighthouse, in the village of Wind Point five miles north of Racine, sits majestically on a small bluff overlooking Lake Michigan. A wide expanse of lush lawn, dotted with a few young hardwoods and pines, brushes up against a white wooden fence and surrounds the two-story dwelling and tower, one of the tallest on the Great Lakes.

A narrow strip around the base of the nearly 110-foot-tall tower is painted gray, and above it a smooth expanse of painted brick stretches skyward in a streak of white. A few small, square windows mark the sides of the conical tower, and in the absence of a keeper, a few have been bricked over. Beneath the lantern room, a circular walkway surrounds a white room with a door providing access. Just beneath the walkway, four arched windows offer views in each direction. The 10-sided lantern room is entirely glazed and is surrounded with its own small, very narrow walkway.

The trim of the tower and attached keeper's house is a gray-green that matches the color of the dwelling's stone basement. The large house has many tall, inviting windows, with graceful curved trim above each on the first story. Several white dormers extend out from the dark-red shingled roof of the second story. An enclosed walkway connects the tower to the house, which also has outside entrances.

Bordering the entire building is a wide cement walkway that, along with a few low-lying shrubs and young bushes planted nearby, gives the house a very crisp, organized profile. The lush lawn stretches down to the water's edge and holds a few benches to provide a relaxing break for visitors. An old tramway that once served the lightstation is now a tumble-down mixture of cement and nearly submerged pilings. The brick whistlehouse sits close to shore, its twin fog horns still positioned out toward the water.

The lighthouse complex is leased by the town of Wind Point and is used as a village hall and police station. A caretaker lives in the house, and the grounds are open to the public. The tower, however, is closed. The Wind Point light still shines, making it one of the oldest still-operational lights on the Great Lakes.

DIRECTIONS: From the intersection of Hwy. 32 (Douglas Ave.) and Three Mile Rd. (about 3.5 driving miles north on Hwy. 32 from Festival Park in Racine) turn right (east) onto Three Mile and go approximately 1.4 miles to where the road jogs left onto Lighthouse Dr. Follow Lighthouse Dr. about 1.2 miles to the driveway to Wind Point lighthouse. As Lighthouse Dr. passes through a golf course, the lighthouse will come into view, ahead and to the right. Upon leaving the golf course, Lighthouse Rd. curves left and passes one house on the right. Just past the house, look for a sign on the right that reads "Wind Point Lighthouse, City Hall, Police Department." Turn right (east) onto the driveway and follow it about 0.2 mile to the parking area.

WIND POINT LIGHTHOUSE

17

Milwaukee Breakwater Lighthouse

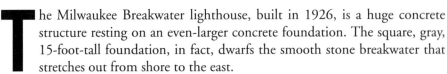

"The foundation dwarfs the smooth stone breakwater."

The Milwaukee Breakwater lighthouse, built in 1926, is a huge concrete structure resting on an even-larger concrete foundation. The square, gray, 15-foot-tall foundation, in fact, dwarfs the smooth stone breakwater that stretches out from shore to the east.

The lighthouse is a large, square two-story building marked with several small, rectangular windows. The tower — symmetrically decorated with identical windows — rises flush with the lower wall two stories above the lighthouse's flat roof, which is enclosed with a sturdy white metal railing. A square walkway surrounds the round black lantern room plus an assortment of antennae that reach even higher skyward.

A small opening splits the breakwater about midway, so it isn't possible to walk all the way out to the light.

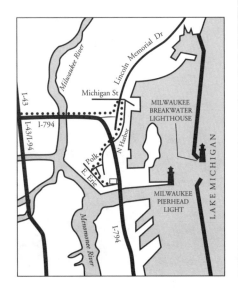

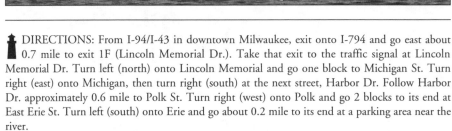

DIRECTIONS: From I-94/I-43 in downtown Milwaukee, exit onto I-794 and go east about 0.7 mile to exit 1F (Lincoln Memorial Dr.). Take that exit to the traffic signal at Lincoln Memorial Dr. Turn left (north) onto Lincoln Memorial and go one block to Michigan St. Turn right (east) onto Michigan, then turn right (south) at the next street, Harbor Dr. Follow Harbor Dr. approximately 0.6 mile to Polk St. Turn right (west) onto Polk and go 2 blocks to its end at East Erie St. Turn left (south) onto Erie and go about 0.2 mile to its end at a parking area near the river.

Turn left into the parking area and park anywhere up to a fence that crosses the lot. Beyond the fence is a designated parking area for senior citizens and the handicapped. Walk through that special area to the water's edge and then make the short trek out to the pierhead light. You can also view the harbor lighthouse from this vantage point.

Milwaukee Pierhead Light

The Milwaukee Pierhead light, at the mouth of the Milwaukee River, was built in 1872 and rebuilt in 1906. The round, red metal-sided tower rests on a pier that stretches out only a short distance from shore. A round, black walkway and lantern room tops the nearly 50-foot-tall structure. Only the front of the lantern room is glazed; metal siding hides the interior at the rear. A small, tightly locked doorway in the base provides access for keepers.

A bright red guardrail along the pier and shoreline invites visitors to stroll its length for a relaxing interlude in bustling Milwaukee.

" A bright red guardrail along the pier and shoreline invites visitors to stroll its length for a relaxing interlude in bustling Milwaukee. "

North Point Lighthouse

" In autumn, when the emerald lawns are dotted with yellow leaves and the pristine white of the tower is brushed with the bright orange of a nearby maple, the scene is exceptionally stunning. "

The first lighthouse to guard the Lake Michigan waters of Milwaukee Bay from North Point was built in 1837. In 1855 it was replaced by the beautiful structure that still stands today. Its massive, octagonal metal tower tapers slightly as it rises, while a band of small windows — some long and narrow, some round — run up each side of the structure.

A ridged joint halfway up the tower resulted from a1912 expansion. Because the light had become difficult to see, a new metal tower was built, and the old tower was raised atop it to nearly double the height. At the parapet an octagonal walkway and lantern room, each painted black, top the structure. A bank of windows surrounding the lantern room provides glimpses of the still-active Fresnel lens inside. A small door with a protective overhang provides access into the tower at ground level, and across a small patch of lawn is the now-boarded-up doorway into the keeper's house.

That building, no longer used as a residence, is a sprawling expanse of white siding and black roofing, with three stories of angles and modern window additions easing the confines of the older home. An ivy-covered fence marks the property lines of the lighthouse grounds, which though now a part of Lake Park are not open to the public.

There is, however, a small visitors area at the north side of the house. An informative sign describes the history of the light, and a statue of a resting lion guides the way to a private walkway that borders a row of bushes before ducking under a willow tree and entering the back yard of the lighthouse complex. There, a long stone driveway is bordered by a dark split-rail fence, and a slender lamp post topped with an ornate globe overlooks the turnaround.

Even though you are kept at a distance, you are affected by the beauty of this light. And in autumn, when the emerald lawns are dotted with yellow leaves and the pristine white of the tower is brushed with the bright orange of a nearby maple, the scene is exceptionally stunning.

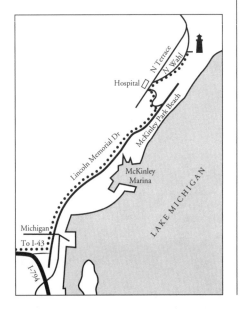

DIRECTIONS: From I-94/I-43 in downtown Milwaukee, exit onto I-794 and go east about 0.7 mile to exit 1F (Lincoln Memorial Dr.). Take that exit to the traffic signal at Lincoln Memorial Dr. Turn left (north) onto Lincoln Memorial and go about 2.0 miles to a traffic signal at an unmarked road (about 0.8 mile north of the Mckinley Marina). Turn left (a right turn leads to the Mckinley Park Beach area) onto the unnamed road, pass the North Point Pumping Station (to the immediate right), and go approximately 0.3 mile to the stop sign on the top of the hill at Terrace Ave. Turn right (north) onto Terrace and go 0.1 mile to North Wahl Ave. Turn right (east) onto Wahl and go about 0.5 mile to the lighthouse driveway, on the right. You will also see the lighthouse, on the right about 200 feet from the road.

NORTH POINT LIGHTHOUSE

NORTH POINT LIGHTHOUSE

Milwaukee's first lighthouse was erected in 1837 on a 56 foot bluff at the east end of Wisconsin Ave. It was replaced in 1855 by a 28 foot tower 100 feet east of the present location. Erosion forced rebuilding in the 1870's and relocation inland. Construction was entirely of bolted cast iron sections. In 1912, a steel plate tower section was built and the iron tower placed on top, giving the light a height of 160 feet above the lake.

The first lantern burned mineral oil. A new lens, installed in 1868 is still in use. The present light source is a 25,000 candlepower lamp rotated electrically and controlled by an automatic time clock. The lens focuses a 1,300,000 candlepower signal visible for 25 miles.

Port Washington Breakwater Light

"A wide arch on each side opens up the area beneath the light."

At the end of a smooth concrete pier, with moss-covered rocks bordering the northern edge, rests the Port Washington Breakwater light, built in 1935. Its concrete foundation is 20 feet tall, and a wide arch on each side opens up the area beneath the light. The white steel tower is centered on this platform, and the square first level includes a doorway with round porthole windows on each side. Above that, the tower — with similar round windows at both the next level and near the top — rapidly tapers upward. A modern red beacon atop the 40-foot-tall structure guides present-day mariners into the harbor of Port Washington.

To the south, a second pier runs out from shore to help form an entrance to the harbor. A small, white cylinder light marks the end of that pier.

The first breakwater light was built here in 1889 to replace an older lighthouse on the bluff back from shore. Built in 1860, the older light was housed in a small tower on the roof of the keeper's house. In 1934 the Coast Guard removed the tower from the dwelling, and in spring 1993 the Port Washington Historical Society was granted a 30-year lease on the 1860 structure for purposes of restoration. Hopefully, the building will eventually be open to the public.

To contact the group, write Light Station Restoration Committee, P.O. Box 491, Port Washington, WI 53074.

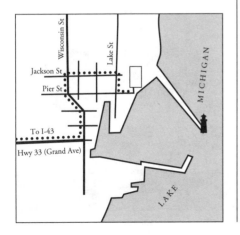

DIRECTIONS: From I-43 north of Milwaukee, take exit # 96 and go east on Hwy. 33 (which changes to Grand Ave.) about 2.9 miles to Wisconsin St., in Port Washington. Turn left (north) onto Wisconsin and go 4 blocks to Jackson St. Turn right (east) onto Jackson and go 3 blocks to Lake St. Turn right (south) onto Lake and go one block to Pier St. Turn left, into the parking area. (Because of limited parking on Jackson St., it is more convenient to park in this area.)

It is about a ¼-mile walk out to the pierhead light on the end of the breakwall.

PORT WASHINGTON BREAKWATER LIGHT

Sheboygan Breakwater Light

The nearly half-mile-long Sheboygan pier angles out from shore north of the Sheboygan Harbor entrance channel. Centering the pier is a wide cement walkway leading directly to the Sheboygan Breakwater light. The center walkway slopes moderately down each side to lower walkways that also stretch the length of the pier. Footing on those lower areas can be treacherous when the sometimes-rough waves of Lake Michigan have washed over them.

The light — a round, red, 30-foot-high metal tower — sits at the end of the pier. Sadly, it's lantern is missing; the round railing at its summit surrounds only a small, modern beacon and a radio antenna.

A park that runs along the shore near the pier has become a final resting place for a few maritime artifacts, including the white oak keel from the *Lottie Cooper*, which sank in 1894 while anchored in the harbor during a fierce storm. Five of the six-man crew were rescued by members of the lifesaving station nearby.

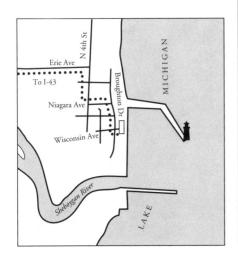

DIRECTIONS: From I-43 just west of Sheboygan, take exit 126 and go east on Hwy 3 (Kohler Memorial Dr.) 1.4 miles to where the divided highway ends. Continue straight, now on Erie Ave., about 1.2 miles to its end at 4th St., in downtown Sheboygan. Turn right (south) onto 4th and go 2 blocks to Niagara Ave. Turn left (east) onto Niagara and go one block to Broughton Dr. Turn right (south) onto Broughton and go 1½ blocks to Wisconsin Ave. Turn left onto Wisconsin and, just past the remains of the *Lottie Cooper*, enter the marina parking area. The breakwater and light are at the north end of the marina, and once there it is a little less than a half-mile walk out to the end of the breakwater.

Manitowoc North Breakwater Lighthouse

Reaching the Manitowoc lighthouse is easy: Just follow the blue railings that mark the smooth half-mile route. The walkway zigzags around the Manitowoc Marina and onto a raised path down the center of a small breakwater. Huge, white boulders line both sides of the pier to create a rough, rugged border out to the mammoth, white lighthouse.

Cement stairs with a black metal handrail lead up from the pier to the light's platform, which is bordered on all sides by a heavy chain draped post to post. Signs warn of the loud fog signal, which sounds without warning. Stenciled onto a bottom corner of the light is "7/16/85 CGC Mesquite." After servicing the light, the crew of the Coast Guard cutter left the routine marking, unaware it would become a small memorial. The ship sank four years later in Lake Superior off Michigan's Keweenaw Peninsula.

The first level of the light is 10 feet tall and is ornamented only by the rows of rivets running up its sides. A slightly smaller second floor rests squarely on the first, its flat roof bordered by a black metal railing. Above the second story, the round tower rises from the center an additional 10 feet. A black railing similar to the one below surrounds the 10-sided lantern room, and a black cap and ventilator ball protect the Fresnel lens inside. The thin line of a radio antenna stretches an additional 20 feet into the air.

Manitowoc, Wisconsin, and Ludington, Michigan, are joined across Lake Michigan by car ferry service. The S.S. *Badger*, the only passenger steam ship on the Great Lakes, makes regular runs through the summer and fall. For more information about this unique trip, call 1-800-841-4243.

Manitowoc also offers a beautiful maritime museum, at the mouth of the Manitowoc River ½ mile from the lighthouse parking area. Detailed exhibits bring to life World War II years, including the experiences of women who rose to new challenges on the home front. Nearby, the World War II submarine the U.S.S. *Cobia* is open for tours.

"Signs warn of the loud fog signal, which could sound without warning."

DIRECTIONS: From I-43 west of Manitowoc, take exit #149 and follow Hwy. 151 to 8th St. in town as follows: From the exit ramp go east on Hwy. 151 about 0.7 mile to where the divided highway ends. Continue straight, now on Calumet Ave., about 1.2 miles to 26th St. Turn left (north) onto 26th and go about 0.1 mile to Custer St. Turn right (east) onto Custer, which changes to Washington St. after one block, and go approximately 1.1 miles to 8th St. Turn left (north) onto 8th and go about 0.5 mile to Maritime Dr., the first street after crossing the drawbridge. Just after turning onto Maritime Dr. you will pass the popular Manitowoc Maritime Museum, on the right. Follow Maritime Dr. about 0.4 mile and turn into the Manitowoc Marina, on the right.

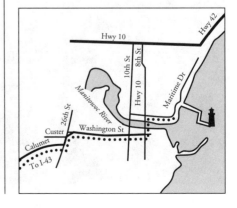

Two Rivers North Pierhead Light Museum

This lighthouse was first built in 1883 on Two Rivers' North Pier. When replaced in 1969 by a steel structure, the old light was given to the town of Two Rivers, and in 1988 the top 15 feet was moved to its present location, on the banks of the East Twin River near the downtown area. That upper section perches atop a modern wood platform supported and elevated 15 feet above the ground by wood legs. Two flights of stairs lead up to a wide deck that surrounds the dark-red, one-story wooden light. At the back side of the square lighthouse, a small but prominent door offers entry, and on each of the other sides, a set of windows illuminates the interior. A small walkway encircles the octagonal, white lantern room, and rectangular windows completely surround the lantern within.

Joined to the lighthouse by a wooden sidewalk and thick rope railing is the Rogers Street Fishing Village Museum, which includes exhibits illustrating the area's nautical history. A wide border of flowering annuals provides a thick slash of color along the walkway, and an anchor from the schooner *America,* sunk in 1880 off Rawley Point, decorates the museum's lawn. The museum is open from 10 a.m. to 4 p.m., June through August. There is a small admission fee.

"The top 15 feet was moved to its present location, on the banks of the East Twin River."

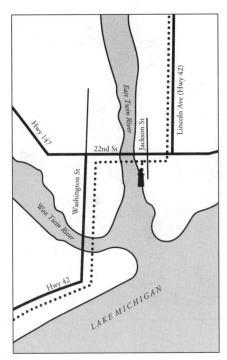

DIRECTIONS: If entering Two Rivers from the south on Hwy. 42, follow 42 north into town as follows: Jog left onto Washington St., which crosses the West Twin River, and go about 0.7 mile to 22nd St. Turn right (east) onto 22nd and go about 0.3 mile to Jackson St., the first street after crossing the bridge over the East Twin River.

If entering Two Rivers from the north on Hwy. 42, follow 42 south to where it jogs right (west) onto 22nd St. and then go 1½ blocks to Jackson St., the last street before crossing the East Twin River.

At Jackson St., turn south and look for the lighthouse and museum, just around the corner on the right. The parking area is across the street from the museum.

Rawley Point Lighthouse

"The three distinctive layers are like a wedding cake."

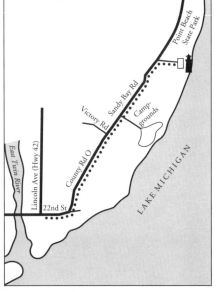

The first light at Rawley Point was lit in 1854, putting an end to numerous tragedies caused by a dangerous shoal extending nearly a mile from shore. In 1894 the tower, which rose from the roof of the keeper's house, was torn down nearly to the roofline and covered over, and a new free-standing tower was constructed nearby.

Still standing, that 111-foot-high steel tower presents an unusual profile. A hollow steel column, just large enough to accommodate a stairway, rises 60 feet to support a much wider circular platform. Surrounded by an ornate railing, that level holds a small room, complete with porthole windows. Above is a second level with railing and then the lantern room with its own small railing. The 10-sided lantern room is only partially glazed; the rear wall is steel painted dark red to match the roof and ventilator ball.

The three distinctive layers are like a wedding cake, a dainty image reinforced by the delicate look of the webbing of white support posts and crossed cables stretching from the top of the pillar to widen out at the bottom. Another unique detail — three gently curved, eight-paned windows are set into each side of the heavy metal column.

Nearby, the brick-red roof of the 2½-story keeper's house matches the tower's lantern room. A charming round turret, the remnants of the original tower, dominates the northern end of the white brick house, adding yet another unusual trait to an already beautiful complex. The surrounding land has been cleared except for a few old hardwoods, and in the distance closer to the Lake Michigan shoreline is the small, white whistle house.

Though surrounded by beautiful Point Beach State Park, the lighthouse is not open to the public. The park offers camping, picnicking, hiking, skiing, nature programs and swimming. A lovely beach stretches along the shore, inviting visitors to go for a dip in the shadow of the guiding light.

DIRECTIONS: From the intersection of Hwy. 42 and 22nd St. in Two Rivers, go east on 22nd (also County Rd. O) about 4 blocks, just past a ball field on the left, to where 22nd St. and County Rd. O) split. Turn left (north), following County Road O (now also Sandy Bay Rd.) about 4.6 miles to the entrance to Point Beach State Park. Turn right (east) and follow the park road about ¼ mile to the registration booth, on the left, where you may purchase a vehicle pass. At this point the lighthouse will be in view, on the right.

RAWLEY POINT LIGHTHOUSE

Kewaunee South Pierhead Lighthouse

The Kewaunee Pierhead lighthouse sits at the end of a flat concrete pier that has been reinforced with steel siding. Set into the west wall of the white two-story house is a wide set of green metal doors three feet off the ground. A catwalk and network of stairs that once provided access to that elevated entry and another above it have been removed. The square, white tower rises about 20 feet above the dark-gray roofline of the house, its square windows now boarded up. The octagonal lantern room, surrounded by a square walkway with black steel railing, still shelters a small Fresnel lens. The tower is capped with a red roof and ventilator ball, and a tall radio antenna rises another 20 feet above.

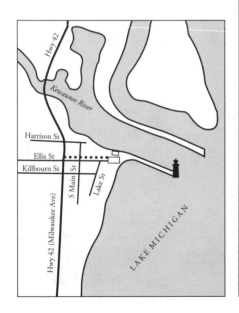

DIRECTIONS: From the intersection of Hwy. 42 and Ellis St., about 0.3 mile south of the Kewaunee River in downtown Kewaunee, turn east onto Ellis and go approximately 0.2 mile to its end. Look for the pier, on the left behind the police station. The lighthouse is at the end of the pier, about ¼ mile out.

Algoma North Pierhead Light

The Algoma Pierhead light, at the mouth of the Ahnapee River, is a round, red metal tower over 50 feet tall. Its first level, dotted with several round porthole windows on all sides, rises 30 feet to a red railing. Above, a slightly smaller section tapers upward another 20 feet, with matching porthole windows peering out over the waters of Lake Michigan. A red lantern room and walkway caps the tower.

The pier that holds the light was built in two separate sections to provide an exit for water that comes in as a result of wave action. The first pier extends from shore 50 feet; the second begins 15 feet to the left, with open water between, then continues another 120 feet out to the pierhead light. A catwalk extends from the end of the first pier across the section of open water, and then stretches down the length of the second pier to join the light.

" The pier that holds the light was built in two separate sections to provide an exit for water."

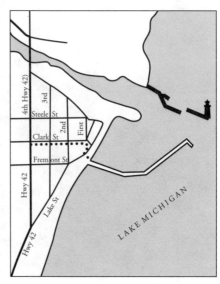

DIRECTIONS: From the intersection of Hwy. 42 and Clark St. in Algoma, go east on Clark 3 blocks, jogging right, to Lake St. Turn right (south) onto Lake and look for the parking area, immediately on your left. Proceed to the south entrance and turn left into it. You can view the light from your car or you can walk north to the marina area to get a better look.

Sturgeon Bay Ship Canal Lighthouse

"Crosshatched panels fill the space between the support posts and cylinder, giving the unique appearance of a garden trellis."

The Sturgeon Bay Coast Guard Station, established on the north side of the entrance to the ship canal in 1899, is an extensive complex that includes three large houses, storage buildings and towering above it all, the Sturgeon Bay Ship Canal lighthouse. All the buildings, including the light tower, have been painted white, and all have dark red roofs. The Lake Michigan shoreline in front of the station has been reinforced with heavy chunks of stone, but farther up the shore, a golden beach stretches along the water's edge. Beautifully manicured lawns carpet the station in emerald green, and huge pines spread their branches all around the property. A delicate border of white chain runs the length of the parking area and driveway, leading the eye toward the light.

The light tower sits 100 yards from the lake on a slight rise. The white steel cylinder rises nearly 100 feet to a circular room that provides support for the black lantern room and walkway above. Large beams angle up the height of the tower to provide support and are connected with a few cross beams for additional stability. At ground level, crosshatched panels fill the space between the support posts and cylinder, giving the unique appearance of a garden trellis ready for a planting of roses.

No visitors are allowed at the operating Coast Guard Station, but there is ample parking near the entrance to the complex, and a path leads down to the pier, which provides a perfect location for photographs.

Sturgeon Bay Ship Canal North Pierhead Light

The North Pierhead light in Sturgeon Bay, Wisconsin, is a three-story square metal building painted brick red. At the second level, a row of square windows peer out from beneath the eaves, and extending from the sharply angled roof of the third story is an entranceway joined by a stairway down to a catwalk.

Standing just in front of that building is the round, red tower, its metal walkway with ornate railing barely extending above the peak of the house's roof. The octagonal lantern room is capped with a red roof and ventilator ball, while an antenna extends even farther skyward.

The approach to the lighthouse is quite unusual, similar to the Algoma Pierhead. A catwalk extends the length of a smooth cement pier, then at the end makes an abrupt left turn and extends across a 20-foot-wide expanse of water to join a second, much-smaller pier that supports the lighthouse. The catwalk ends at the small stairway that provides access to the house's third-level door.

"The approach to the lighthouse is quite unusual."

DIRECTIONS: From the intersection of Hwy. 42/57 and Utah St. at the eastern edge of Sturgeon Bay (0.7 miles north of the modern bridge over the Sturgeon Bay Canal and marked by a sign to the U.S. Coast Guard Station), go east on Utah about 0.4 mile, following the curve to the right onto Cove Rd., and then go approximately 0.3 mile farther to Canal Dr. Turn left onto Canal and drive about 2.6 miles to the U.S. Coast Guard Station. The parking area is on the right, just before entering the station.

The trail to the pierhead light is straight ahead through the entrance to the Coast Guard Station. This is an active station and you must stay on the trail to the pier and not wander onto Coast Guard property. It's not necessary; you can get good views of both the lighthouse and pierhead light from the entrance road and the pier itself. The area is open to the public from sunrise to sunset.

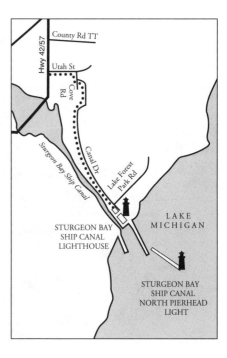

Baileys Harbor Front Range Light and Rear Range Lighthouse

" The rear range light was once used as a parsonage. "

Baileys Harbor Front Range light, built in 1869, is a small, white two-story structure near the Lake Michigan shoreline. Small, delicately arched windows illuminate the interior of the first story, and the entryway — a wood platform and door — is painted dark hunter green. The square first story changes to an octagonal second level, with small triangles of green roofing covering each corner that has narrowed. A small window on the upper level provides a view of the beacon from the lake, and the structure is capped with a green metal roof and ventilator ball.

Inland about ¼ mile is the Baileys Harbor Rear Range light, now a private residence. The former keeper's house is a pretty two-story wooden dwelling, its red-shingled roof topped with a square cupola whose lone small, arched window overlooks the blue waters of Lake Michigan where once the rear range shone forth. The roof of the small front porch has unusual supports — several beams

BAILEYS HARBOR REAR RANGE LIGHTHOUSE

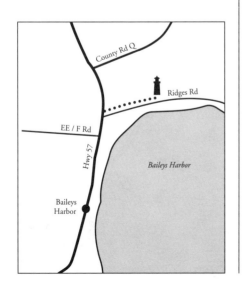

DIRECTIONS: From the intersection of Hwy. 57 and Ridges Rd. (0.2 miles north of County Rd. EE/F and 0.4 mile south of County Rd. Q on the north side of Baileys Harbor), turn east onto Ridges Rd. and go about 0.3 mile to the front range light, on the left.

Although the Rear Range lighthouse is a private residence, you can get a good view of it by walking the trail through the park property directly behind the Front Range light.

that branch off to each side as they reach the overhang, creating a treelike effect.

This light was once used as a parsonage. Lutheran pastors lived here between 1930 and 1955 and kept both range lights as part of the agreement for using the property. This is still private property that must be respected, but you can take good pictures from the public trail leading back to the rear range lighthouse.

Both lights are on the National Register of Historic Places.

"Small, delicately arched windows illuminate the interior of the front range."

BAILEYS HARBOR FRONT RANGE LIGHT

Old Baileys Harbor Lighthouse Ruins

"The unusually long, dome-shaped skeleton, now bereft of glass, resembles a delicate bird cage."

The 144-year-old Old Baileys Harbor light, on private Lighthouse Island, rests close to the shoreline of Lake Michigan, nearly hidden by a surrounding stand of pines and cedars. Farther north, white birch contrast with the darkness of the forest running along the shoreline, and a few low rock outcroppings serve to blunt the force of the waves.

The 40-foot-tall, round light tower, made of light-colored rocks, peeks out from behind the screen of green, topped by its now-empty lantern room. The unusually long, dome-shaped skeleton, now bereft of glass, resembles a delicate bird cage. Almost completely hidden in the trees are the remains of a building, possibly the former dwelling. Close to the shoreline at the tower's base sits a small, white, square building, its fresh coat of paint contrasting starkly with the ruins behind it.

This lighthouse became obsolete when the new set of range lights were built for the harbor in 1869. It is doubtful whether this light will survive much longer unless steps are quickly taken to stabilize what is left of this once-proud landmark.

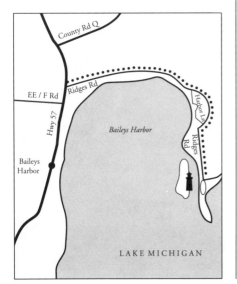

DIRECTIONS: From the intersection of Hwy. 57 and Ridges Rd. (0.2 miles north of County Rd. EE/F and 0.4 mile south of County Rd. Q on the north side of Baileys Harbor), turn east onto Ridges Rd. and go about 1.5 miles to where Ridges Rd. curves to the left at Harbor Ln. Continue on Ridges about ½ mile to where it again junctions with Harbor Ln. Again, stay on Ridges Rd. and go another ½ mile to its end. Drive straight ahead off of the blacktop into the large open area where you will get a good view of the old, abandoned lighthouse, on an island off to the right.

Cana Island Lighthouse

The Cana Island lighthouse setting is among the most beautiful of lighthouses anywhere. From the parking area, a short hike across a low-lying stone causeway brings you to the tiny island. There, a low, white limestone wall surrounds most of the lighthouse. Oscar Knutson, a keeper of the light, spent a year from 1919 to 1920 building up the impressive wall from stones he gathered at the shoreline. In 1921 he devoted a week to building a pair of 3-foot-tall pillars that frame a small opening in the wall and mark the entrance to a path to the base of the tower. During the remainder of his stay here, Knutson continued improving his beautiful, delicate wall, now covered here and there by the branches of fragrant cedars.

The light tower, built in 1869, is more than 80 feet tall, and the original brick tower is now protected with sheet metal, with scores of rivets outlining each section. A few porthole windows gaze out over the water, and at the top, decorative posts support a circular room with a doorway opening out onto a surrounding walkway. Above, the 10-sided lantern room sparkles in the sunlight, except for a few panels on the north side that are steel instead of glass. Capped by a domed copper roof now green with exposure to the weather, the lantern room still houses an active Fresnel lens.

Attached to the base of the tower is the two-story yellow brick keeper's dwelling, which was home to two families at a time. A distinctive three-flue chimney rises from the peak of the bright red roof, and a small addition angles off from the back of the house. The structure provides a colorful backdrop for the plantings of flowers and shrubs along its base.

The surrounding lawn is broken only by a few medium-size trees, and behind the house, two interesting buildings remain from bygone days. A six-sided, white-stone well building rests near a white brick outhouse, both topped with a red roof matching that of the dwelling. Cedars stretch out from the forest in a vain attempt to scale a low stone wall behind the buildings.

Today, the still-operating lighthouse complex is licensed to the Door County Maritime Museum, and the grounds are open daily from 10 a.m. to 5 p.m., except that picnics are not allowed. The dwelling is a private residence, and so visitors are urged to abide by the time frame listed above.

"The Cana Island lighthouse setting is among the most beautiful of lighthouses anywhere."

DIRECTIONS: From the intersection of Hwy. 57 and County Rd. Q north of Baileys Harbor, turn east onto CR-Q and go 3.5 miles to Cana Island Rd. Turn right (south) onto Cana Island Rd. and go about 0.1 mile to a T intersection. Turn right and, following the signs to the Spike Horn Campgrounds, continue on Cana Island Rd. one mile to Boes Point Rd., (a gravel road) going straight ahead. Jog sharply left, staying on Cana Island Rd. another 1.2 miles to its end. (At ½ mile the road passes through the Spikehorn Campground and near its end passes Cana Cove Rd., a gravel road on the left.)

Park on the roadside before the blacktop ends and then walk to the end of the road and across the old causeway to the island. This area can be water-covered, so wear old shoes. On the island, follow the trail to the left about 1½ blocks to the lighthouse grounds.

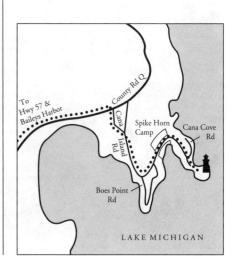

CANA ISLAND LIGHTHOUSE

Potawatomi Lighthouse

uilt in 1836, the Potawatomi lighthouse is now part of Wisconsin's beautiful Rock Island State Park in Lake Michigan. The light was rebuilt in 1858 after a fierce storm swept it from its precarious hold near the shore. The massive, square structure is made of roughly shaped, light-tan stone, the narrow rectangular blocks creating a foot-thick wall strong enough to withstand nearly anything nature can throw at it. The sides are adorned with tall, elegant eight-paned windows bordered in white and topped with small, graceful stone arches. A small attic window is similarly designed, and the walkout basement also has three similar openings, but they are now boarded up and it is unclear whether they were doors or windows. In the 1850s the basement served as a school, filled with children from a nearby fishing village who were taught by

"In the 1850s the basement served as a school, filled with children taught by an assistant keeper's wife."

"A large, window-lined room with several French doors opens onto a wide terrace."

an assistant keeper's wife. The shiny, dark-red tile roof reflects a large chimney built of different-colored bricks, creating a simple, yet beautiful visual effect.

The square, white tower rises from the front of the house but barely tops the roofline before the walkway widens out to a surrounding black metal railing. Unfortunately, the entire lantern room has been removed, leaving an all-too-familiar sad, gaping space.

Added on to the back of the house is a one-story, wood-sided room roofed in dark red tile to match that of the larger stone structure. White paint that covered its siding has faded away to gray in large sections. Nearby, an old stone wellhouse lies nearly hidden in an overgrowth of trees. The half-buried well is still open, so exercise caution in this area.

To reach Rock Island, we took a small passenger ferry from Washington Island. Near the dock on the island, a huge, modern boathouse topped by the Great Hall — a large, window-lined room with several French doors opening onto a wide terrace — stands as a reminder of the plans wealthy inventor C.H. Thordarson had for creating a fabulous estate on the island during the 1920s. But though Thordarson lived another 20 years, the boathouse was the only substantial structure ever built.

Today, the spectacular Great Hall has an informative historical display inside, and the beauty of its floor-to-ceiling windows, hand-carved furniture and shining hardwood floors are worth a visit. The state park also offers camping and picnicking, but no wheeled vehicles (bikes, strollers, etc.) can be used on the island, except for a few used by park personnel.

A one-mile trail leads from the ferry dock over hills and through beautiful wooded areas out to the light. A few side paths branch off to the right, but to get to the lighthouse, always stay on the left trail.

The lighthouse will eventually be restored with the help of funding from private donations as well as the Wisconsin State Historical Society, the National Parks Service, and the Department of Natural Resources. An active local group, Friends of Rock Island State Park, devotes much time and energy to the project. You may write them at 126 Country Club Drive, Clintonville, WI 54929.

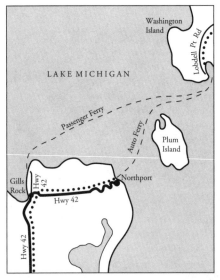

DIRECTIONS: To visit the Potawatomi lighthouse on Rock Island you must first take a car ferry from Northport to Washington Island and then a passenger ferry to Rock Island State Park.

To get to the car ferry to Washington Island, go north on Hwy. 42 to Gills Rock. At the north end of town, Hwy. 42 goes both straight ahead (north) and also to the right (east). (The route north leads to a passenger ferry to Washington Island.) Follow Hwy. 42 to the right (east) about two miles to the auto ferry dock, at the road's end in Northport. From the ferry you will get a distant view of the Pilot Island lighthouse and a fine view of the Plum Island Range lighthouse and Life Saving Service Installation.

From the ferry dock on Washington Island, drive straight ahead (north) on Lobdell Point Rd. about 1.7 miles as it bears east to Main Rd. Turn left (north) onto Main and go approximately 2.5 miles to Jackson Harbor Rd. Turn right (east) onto Jackson Harbor Rd. and drive about 3.6 miles to where it turns left at Old Camp Rd. Follow Jackson Harbor Rd. to the left (north) 0.3 mile to where it jogs right (east) into Jackson Harbor. Don't turn; continue straight ahead about 0.1 mile to the Rock Island Ferry dock, on the right.

From the dock on Rock Island, walk left about one block to a stone building on the hill. Follow the trail behind the building up the hill to a large timber arch. From this point you follow the trail, a good two-track road, approximately one mile to the lighthouse. Along the route, several paths go off to the right, but always stay left, along the bluff with Lake Michigan just off to the left.

For Washington Island and Rock Island ferry schedules, fees and other information, contact Washington Island, Rock Island Ferry, Main Road, Washington Island, Wisconsin 54246; (414) 847-2252.

Plum Island Range Lighthouse

Where Green Bay meets Lake Michigan, the perilous waters were often referred to as *Porte des Mortes* — "Death's Door." Part of the reason are shoals extending one third of a mile out from Plum Island, the largest island in the entrance to Green Bay.

Helping to mark that dangerous area is the Plum Island Rear Range lighthouse, built in 1897 about 100 yards from shore on the island's gently sloping terrain. The white steel tower consists of a center cylinder surrounded by metal supports stretching from beneath the first walkway down to the ground. Atop the cylinder, a larger circular room is surrounded by a walkway, while above it the slightly smaller lantern room protects the still-working light.

Near the tower, a beautiful brick keeper's house is nestled closer to the thick forest behind. Constructed of light-brown brick and roofed in dark red shingles, its natural colors blend in with the dark greens of the surrounding forest. And small pines that dot the large lawn, no longer strictly maintained, are surrounded by the golds and greens of tall wild grasses.

A wide path cleared through the thick forest leads about 300 yards to the Front Range light, a small, white skeleton tower nearly touching the beach on the southeast shore of the island.

Dominating a small strip of land on the north side of the island is a lifesaving station. A large dwelling there is complete with its own watch tower rising just above the roofline. At the water's edge is a boathouse, with room enough for three rescue vessels. Pilings from long-unused docks stand in the blue waters as quiet reminders of a once-bustling, and essential nautical station. A Coast Guard Station is still operated seasonally at this location.

"The perilous waters were often referred to as Porte des Mortes – 'Death's Door.'"

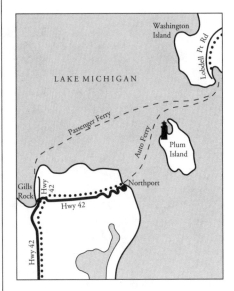

DIRECTIONS: You can get fine views of the Plum Island Range lighthouse and Life Saving Service Installation from the auto ferry connecting Northport to Washington Island.

To get to the ferries, go north on Hwy. 42 to Gills Rock. At the north end of town, Hwy. 42 goes both straight ahead (north) and also to the right (east). The route north leads to the passenger ferry. To get to the auto ferry, follow Hwy. 42 to the right (east) about two miles to the road's end in Northport.

For the ferries' schedules, fees and other information, contact Washington Island, Rock Island Ferry, Main Road, Washington Island, Wisconsin 54246; (414) 847-2252.

Pilot Island Lighthouse

"*Pilot Island is a small stroke of green against the deep turquoise waters of Lake Michigan.*"

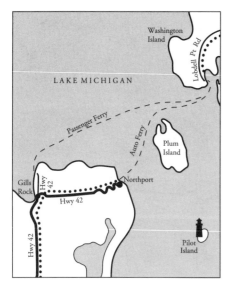

◆ DIRECTIONS: You can get a distant view of the Pilot Island lighthouse from the auto ferry connecting Northport to Washington Island.

To get to the ferries, go north on Hwy. 42 to Gills Rock. At the north end of town, Hwy. 42 goes both straight ahead (north) and also to the right (east). The route north leads to the passenger ferry. To get to the auto ferry, follow Hwy. 42 to the right (east) about two miles to the road's end in Northport.

For the ferries' schedules, fees and other information, contact Washington Island, Rock Island Ferry, Main Road, Washington Island, Wisconsin 54246; (414) 847-2252.

Pilot Island is a small stroke of green against the deep turquoise waters of Lake Michigan two miles out from the Door Peninsula. Pines and cedars, with a smattering of hardwoods, cover the island, and the rocky shoreline still guards the island well.

Leading from shore near the long-forgotten remains of a crumbling dock is a path to a two-story lightkeeper's house, built in 1858 in the midst of a small, cleared area. Made of light-tan brick, the dwelling has several elongated windows, each with an arch of white trim above. The dark red roof supports the light tower, which rises just above the peak to a black, 10-sided lantern room and square walkway.

During the early 1880s, the assistant keeper here was Martin Knudson who, after a brief stint as lightkeeper at Michigan's South Manitou Island, returned to Pilot Island as head lightkeeper. During his years on the island, Knudson saved several lives. During a violent October 1892 storm, for instance, Knudson, with the help of his assistant keepers, rescued the crews of two schooners — the *J.R. Gillmore* and the *A.P. Nichols* — that had run aground off the island. Knudson's courageous actions earned him medals from both the Life Saving Benevolent Association of New York and the government of the United States of America.

Eagle Bluff Lighthouse Museum

The Eagle Bluff lighthouse was built on a 50-foot cliff overlooking Lake Michigan in 1868. The keeper's house and tower are constructed of light-tan bricks, as are the oil building and small outhouse nearly hidden in the trees. The two-story keeper's house is chock-full of square, 12-paned windows, each with a pair of hunter green shutters ready to ward off even the most bitter winter gale. A one-story room whose roof angles down out of the south side has its own entry door and a low window overlooking a beautiful border of marigolds in the summer. The roofs of this room and the main dwelling are both shingled in dark red, their steep angles made more pronounced by a border of white eaves with decorative supporting arches. A cross bar with spire decorates each gable.

The heavy, square tower dominates the northeastern corner of the house and is joined at an angle. A small, square window with white, arched trim marks the tower halfway up on the front, while an identical window sits just below the square, black iron walkway on another side. The 10-sided lantern room is entirely glazed, except for two panels to the rear that are sheathed in metal. A bright red cap and ventilator ball provide the finishing touches for this beautiful tower and home.

The spacious grounds surrounding the lighthouse invite you to stroll around the area. On two sides, narrow cement walkways are bordered by white gravel and huge lilac bushes that shade the path. As the sidewalks disappear, a path of the white gravel continues, winding past the tower and down to a low stone wall overlooking the lake. An anchor from the ship *Oakleaf*, which sank in 1926 in Sturgeon Bay after 60 years of service, rests ceremoniously on the front lawn, cordoned off with a heavy, black chain draped between four corner posts.

The site has been restored by the Door County Historical Society with assistance from the United States Coast Guard and the Department of Natural Resources and is open to the public. For a small fee you can tour the keeper's house, which is open daily from Memorial Day to the third week in October, 10 a.m. to 5 p.m. A picnic area and restrooms are near the asphalt parking area.

The lighthouse is a part of the Peninsula State Park, which encompasses 3,700 acres, much of it undeveloped, and offers hiking, biking, golf, folk theater, fishing and swimming. A state park entrance fee is charged.

"The two-story keeper's house is chock-full of square, 12-paned windows, each with a pair of hunter green shutters ready to ward off even the most bitter winter gale."

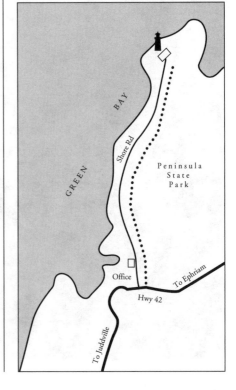

DIRECTIONS: From Hwy. 42 near the center of the town of Fish Creek, about midway between Juddville and Ephriam, turn north into Peninsula State Park and proceed about 0.2 mile to the office. After paying the entrance fee and picking up a park map, continue straight ahead and follow Shore Rd. approximately 4 miles to the lighthouse parking area, on the left.

Chambers Island Lighthouse

"The beautiful tower has a distinctive design."

Chambers Island guards the passage into western Green Bay, and its lighthouse dominates the northwest shore. The keeper's dwelling is a two-story brick structure topped by a reddish-brown roof with white trim and wood cross bars at the gables. The beautiful tower, attached to the northeast corner of the house, has a distinctive design that tapers the corners of the square first level inward to become octagonal at the second level.

This lighthouse is no longer in service, and its lack of use is apparent. Although still in relatively good condition, windows have been boarded up, creating black splotches across the face of the yellow brick, and the top of the octagonal tower has lost its lantern room.

A modern steel skeleton light has been built nearby, with diamond-shaped red-and-white day markers at its top. A cleared area surrounding both lights sweeps down from a slight rise to touch the gravelly beach of Green Bay and provides a slight break to the vast hardwood forest covering the island.

Sherwood Point Lighthouse

" The Sherwood Point lighthouse was the last American lighthouse on the Great Lakes to be manned."

The Sherwood Point lighthouse was the last American lighthouse on the Great Lakes to be manned, its final keeper leaving in the fall of 1983, the lighthouse's centennial year. Its red brick keepers dwelling and attached white brick light tower, however, still survey the waters of Lake Michigan off the point.

When the light was first built, in 1883, the basement had to be blasted from bedrock. And when its fourth-order Fresnel lens was lit, it could sometimes be seen 18 miles across Green Bay in Menominee, Michigan.

In the 1890s the light was kept by William Cochems, one of many keepers who performed their duties here with unflinching loyalty. From 1898 to 1929, Cochems had a special assistant who was dear to his heart — his wife Minnie. And when she died, her faithful, loving husband immortalized her and her service by building a small monument that still rests close to the light.

Today, the Sherwood Point lighthouse is used as a private residence by the Coast Guard. Visitors are discouraged, and the only acceptable way to view it is from the water.

Peshtigo Reef Light

Built in 1934, the Peshtigo Reef light is three miles offshore from Peshtigo Point, surrounded by the deep turquoise waters of Green Bay. It warns navigators of a dangerous reef extending three miles out from the light and lying a dangerous one to six feet below the surface. The structure's round concrete foundation is reinforced with metal siding, and the round base of the tower is centered on that platform. A few small, square windows peer out from the base across the unbroken expanse of water, but the narrower tower, with its beam 72 feet above the water, has only a few porthole windows just beneath the black walkway and lantern room. A thick, red stripe bisects the white tower, providing a visual aid to ships passing by.

"The light warns navigators of a dangerous reef."

Green Bay Harbor Entrance Light

Nine miles offshore, the Green Bay Harbor Entrance light rests on a round concrete foundation 15 feet above the rough waters. On the center of the foundation, a round, white one-story metal room supports the slender light tower, which rises an additional 40 feet and is topped with a modern beacon and radio antenna.

41

Long Tail Point Light Ruins

The grassy banks of Long Tail Point are broken only by the stony ruins of a long-forgotten light. Only the tower remains — its lantern room, walkway, and even windows and doors have long since perished. The strength of its construction has left the remaining shell remarkably intact, a reminder of the history and danger along this flat and unassuming peninsula.

Grassy Island Range Lights

The Grassy Island Range lights have been saved from destruction by the farsighted members of the Green Bay Yacht Club, who moved the structures from their offshore home to the group's headquarters near the mouth of the Fox River.

The white wood shingles that cover the sides of the square Outer light are broken only by a few square windows with black trim. A wide metal walkway and railing have been attached to the sides of the structure about 20 feet above the ground, and the wooden walls of the tower rise above the walkway to support the octagonal lantern room. A black metal cap and large ventilator ball complete the rustic light tower.

Nearby stands the Inner Range light, its square, white tower angling slightly as it rises. Horizontal wood siding covers the structure, and a single window looks out over the parking area. Similar to the Outer Range, a walkway has been attached to the sides of the tower, which continues to rise to support the octagonal lantern room.

REAR RANGE

FRONT RANGE

DIRECTIONS: From I-43 in Green Bay, take exit #187 (Webster Ave.), the first exit east of the bridge over the Fox River. If coming from the west, turn left onto Webster (which changes to East Shore Dr.) and follow it about 0.5 mile to the traffic signal at Bay Beach Rd. If coming from the east, make a right-hand turn onto Webster (which changes to East Shore Dr.) and go about 0.1 mile to the traffic signal at Bay Beach Rd.

Turn left (north) onto Bay Beach Rd. and go about 1.2 miles, as it turns west to its end at a stop sign. Look for the lights to the left, across a parking area, near the Fox River and the U.S. Coast Guard station. Turn left (south) at the stop sign and go approximately 0.2 miles to the large public parking area on the right. Although the lights are on private property, you will have a very good view from the parking area.

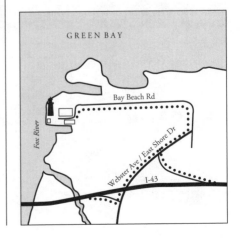

Ashland Breakwater Light

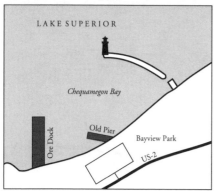

The Ashland Breakwater light rests at the end of a rugged mile-long breakwater stretching out into Lake Superior. A row of rectangular windows runs up each side of the square, white tower, which narrows slightly toward a circular room directly beneath the lantern room. Inside, a modern beacon helps ships make the safety of Ashland Harbor.

Surrounding the light are the waters of Chequamegon Bay, and beyond, the beautiful deep green hills of Ashland lie terraced in the background.

DIRECTIONS: On US-2 in Ashland, drive to Bayview Park (about 0.7 mile east of a large iron ore dock extending into the harbor). Because this light is on a detached breakwater you can't walk to it, but fairly good views come from the park. The best views come from the water.

Apostle Islands Lighthouses

*A*s the glaciers finally receded from the Lake Superior shoreline, they left in their slow-moving wakes a cluster of islands off Wisconsin's Bayfield Peninsula.

Early Native Americans, however, attributed the birth of these islands to the first man who walked the earth. He was chasing a buck, and when the deer outdistanced him, the disappointed hunter grabbed a handful of thick earth and flung it after the disappearing animal. Where each clod of dirt fell, an island appeared as a flash of emerald in the once-empty expanse of Lake Superior blue.

The stunning beauty of the Apostle Islands National Lakeshore, which was created in 1970 and today includes 21 of the 22 islands in the archipelago, makes it one of the most popular destinations on the Great Lakes. Boaters, hikers, campers and photographers are all captivated by the Lake Superior gems.

But the pull of the area is even stronger for lighthouse enthusiasts. The National Park Service has made a solid commitment to the preservation of the eight lighthouses — Chequamegon Point, LaPointe, Michigan Island Old and New, Raspberry Island, Outer Island, Devils Island and Sand Island — within the park's boundaries. The Raspberry Island lighthouse is now a museum, with tours of the facility conducted by a 1920s-acting lightkeeper. All of the park's lighthouses are accessible by tour boat or water taxi, depending on weather and prior reservations.

There are two departure points for Apostle Islands Cruise Service tours. The *Island Princess* leaves from the city dock in Bayfield, and the *Sea Queen II* leaves from Little Sand Bay. (Maps and directions, page 57.) Available are sunset cruises, photography cruises and special cruises tailored to lighthouse enthusiasts. One of the most popular trips is the Grand Tour, a daily three-hour narrated cruise that passes 19 of the 22 Apostle Islands.

Private charters are also available aboard either a Zodiac (a 16-foot inflatable boat) or a larger water taxi that will carry up to six adults. For more information on cruise schedules and the private charters, contact Apostle Islands Cruise Service, P.O. Box 691, Bayfield, Wisconsin 54814; (715) 779-3925.

When visiting the area, stop first at the National Park Service Visitor Center in Bayfield to get up-to-date information on special programs such as guided tours of the Raspberry Island lighthouse and Manitou Island Fish Camp, and walking tours with naturalists on Sand Island and Stockton Island. Also inside the Visitors Center is a small museum with displays of local artifacts plus the Fresnel lens from the Michigan Island lighthouse.

For further information on the park area, contact the Apostle Islands National Lakeshore, Rte. 1, Box 4, Bayfield, Wisconsin 54814; (715) 779-3397.

" Native Americans attributed the birth of these islands to the first man who walked the earth."

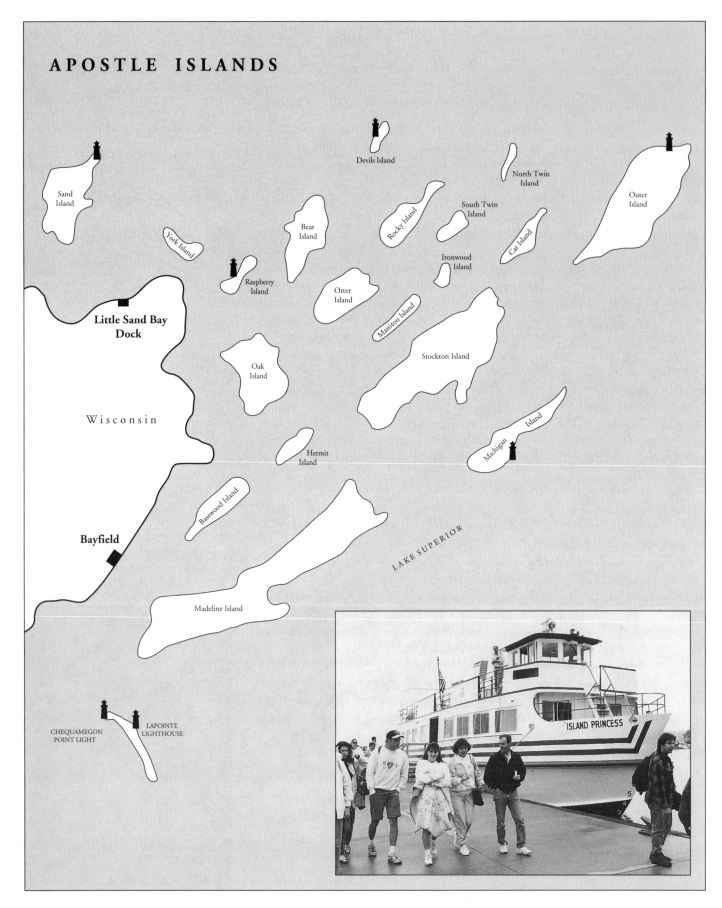

APOSTLE ISLANDS

Sand
Island

Devils Island

North Twin
Island

Outer
Island

York Island

Bear
Island

Rocky Island

South Twin
Island

Cat Island

Raspberry
Island

Ironwood
Island

Otter
Island

Little Sand Bay
Dock

Manitou Island

Oak
Island

Stockton Island

Wisconsin

Michigan   Island

Hermit
Island

Basswood Island

Bayfield

LAKE SUPERIOR

Madeline Island

CHEQUAMEGON
POINT LIGHT

LAPOINTE
LIGHTHOUSE

ISLAND PRINCESS

5
3

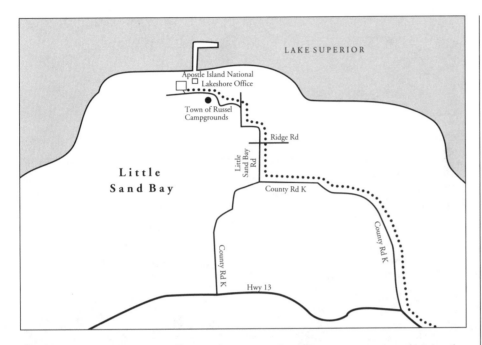

DIRECTIONS: From downtown Bayfield, go north on Hwy. 13 approximately 5.3 miles, bearing west to the junction with County Road K. (Just before this junction you will see a sign that reads "Apostle Islands National Lakeshore Sand Bay Campgrounds 8 miles.") Turn right (north) onto County Road K and go about 5 miles, bearing west, to Little Sand Bay Rd. (Just before this junction, you will see another sign pointing to the campgrounds, 3 miles ahead.) Turn right (north) onto Little Sand Bay Rd. and go about 3 miles to the National Lakeshore Office, on the right as you enter the campgrounds area. Go just past the building and turn right into the parking area. You will board the cruise boat just north of the parking area in the marina.

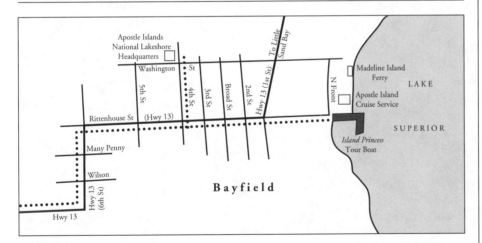

DIRECTIONS: Entering Bayfield from the south, follow Hwy. 13 as it turns left (north) onto Sixth St. and then follow Sixth St. 3 blocks to Rittenhouse St. To visit the Apostle Islands National Lakeshore Visitor Center, turn right (east) onto Rittenhouse and go 2 blocks to 4th St. Turn left (north) onto 4th and go one block to Washington St. Look for the National Lakeshore Visitor Center (a large, red stone building) across the street to the left. Continue across Washington and park behind the building.

To get to the Apostle Islands Cruise Service from the visitor center, return on 4th to Rittenhouse. Turn left (east) onto Rittenhouse (Hwy. 13) and go 3 blocks to where Hwy. 13 jogs left onto 1st St. Continue straight ahead on Rittenhouse (now one-way) one more block to Front St. The Apostle Islands Cruise service is just across Front St. in the large white building on the left. It is best to either park on Rittenhouse before you reach Front or turn left onto Front, park and walk to the cruise service office.

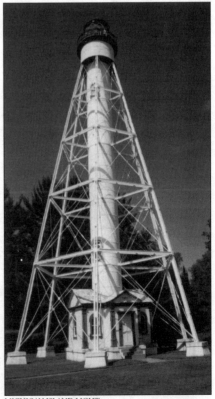

MICHIGAN ISLAND LIGHT

Chequamegon Point Light

The light at Chequamegon Point, built in 1896 on the western shore of Long Island, is nearly hidden by wild pines that surround it and run up to a narrow strip of sand. The square, white steel-sided room rests on four thin legs, and the 42-foot-tall structure ends at the red roof and ventilator ball capping its octagonal lantern room.

In 1987 the tower was moved back 150 feet from the eroding shoreline in a successful effort to protect the light

Nearby and five feet shorter is a modern cylinder light whose beacon and fog signal provide guidance for area boaters.

La Pointe Light

The La Pointe lightstation, on the north shore of Long Island, was first built in 1858 to protect mariners from the area's shoals and a sandbar. The La Pointe light that stands today was built in 1896 along with the tower on Chequamegon Point.

Metal supports and bracing surround the white steel cylindrical tower, and at its top, just above the treetops is a 10-sided walkway and railing surrounding an enclosed circular room. Above it is the octagonal lantern room, surrounded with its own smaller railing. The 67-foot-tall structure is capped by a red ventilator ball with a weathervane balanced on its top. A modern green beacon now assists navigators through this stretch of Lake Superior.

Adjacent buildings and rusty remnants of an old dock nearby were part of this Coast Guard Station but are no longer used.

Thick jack pines on both sides of the light stop just short of the sandy beach, leaving room for dune grasses to gain a foothold, while bleached driftwood lies scattered along the water's edge.

Blueberry pickers flock to the island in July, but beware: the area is also home to a vigorous growth of poison ivy.

> *"Thick pines stop just short of the sandy beach, leaving room for dune grasses to gain a foothold."*

Michigan Island Old Lighthouse Michigan Island Light

"This was no ordinary construction-site confusion, but rather a monumental mix-up."

MICHIGAN ISLAND LIGHT

MICHIGAN ISLAND OLD LIGHTHOUSE

Visitors to the Michigan Island lighthouses are first greeted by spectacularly huge, gorgeous red-clay bluffs lining the shore in front of the complex. Fifty yards back from the bluffs' edge stands the old Michigan Island lighthouse, a quaint two-story home constructed in 1857 of whitewashed stone interrupted by a recessed doorway and green-shuttered windows. A charming dormer window peeks out from the roof, which has taken on a yellow hue from moss growing on the shingles. The dark green trim along the eaves and around the windows blends beautifully with the surrounding thick forest.

The circular stone tower, also painted white, rises to support a black steel walkway and 10-sided lantern room, which originally housed a 3½-order Fresnel lens, now on display in the Apostle Islands National Lakeshore Visitor Center in Bayfield.

Construction of this light began in confusion — and not ordinary construction-site confusion, but a monumental mix-up. The lighthouse was supposed to be built on nearby Long Island, but instead was built here. After the beacon had been lit, an inspector realized the mistake, but the Lighthouse Service allowed the light to be used until the end of the shipping season. The lantern room was then removed and moved to the structure at Windmill Point on Lake St. Clair. But later, a light *was* needed on Michigan Island and in 1869, after the addition of a new $6,000 lantern room, a beacon again shone here.

Sixty-one years later, the lighthouse was displaced and made obsolete by the structure still standing just a few yards west. That huge, white steel tower originally guarded the waters off Schooner Ledge, on the Delaware River at the outskirts of Philadelphia, but was taken down in 1916. In 1929 it was reassembled and lit on Michigan Island. The cylindrical tower — supported by a web of steel beams and wires — rises 112 feet, making it one of the tallest lights on the Great Lakes. At the center of the base of the narrow center cylinder sits a small building, its arched windows and intricately carved corner supports providing an unusual contrast to the modern-looking structure surrounding it. Only a few arched windows illuminate the interior of the tower, and a circular room perched atop supports the black metal walkway and lantern room. The entire lantern room is glazed, and you can glimpse sections of blue sky through the crosshatched panes, which are the perfect finishing touch for this attractive light.

Lush lawns encircle both towers, keeping the forest at bay and providing an inviting carpet for visitors. A combination tramway/ 96-step stairway leads up the side of the bluff from the water's edge to the lawn.

Raspberry Island Lighthouse Museum

" Raspberry Island is one of the few places where you can actually see what an active turn-of-the-century lighthouse must have been like. "

PARK RANGER MATT WELTER IN HIS ROLE AS HERBERT "TOOTS" WINFIELD, LIGHTKEEPER AT RASPBERRY ISLAND 1922-1930.

The Raspberry Island Light Station overlooks Lake Superior from atop a small bluff on the island's southwest shore. The red sands of the hillside — stabilized in many places by grass and bushes — spill down to the shore, where a long row of rock piles have lessened the effects of wave erosion. A small, L-shaped wood dock stretches out a few yards from shore, and a white boathouse perches just above the water's surface. The Apostle Islands ferry from Bayfield drops visitors off at the dock, and returns in two hours for the trip back.

From the dock, a steep combination stairway/tram climbs the hillside to the whistlehouse. The red-brick, single-story building is trimmed in a deep hunter green, including shutters bordering the windows. Delicate white arches top the windows and doorway, and a large dormer extends from the red roof. White trim around the dormer window and down its corners as well as along the eaves and drain pipes adds a distinctive outline to this building.

Just yards north is the main attraction — the spectacular Raspberry Island lighthouse. The huge, white two-story wooden building, built in 1863, is fronted by a wide porch resting on a red brick foundation with large, white vents. Heavy, square pillars rise up to support an overhang, and a gray railing runs along the front.

The square light tower, with its own entryway, bisects the porch. The 46-foot tower rises just above the house's red metal roof to a walkway that widens out to support the 10-sided black metal lantern room. Its Fresnel lens has been removed and is now in the Madeline Island Museum.

In 1906 the dwelling underwent major renovation and remodling into a triplex, with living quarters for the head lightkeeper on one side and an apartment for each of the two assistants on the other. Since the house was constructed for use by more than one family, separate stairways climb up the front porch on each side of the tower to their own entrance door. Similarly in the rear of the building, twin sets of steps lead up to two back doors, each protected with an overhang covered with red shingles. There are even two outhouses.

A collection of long, rectangular, black-trimmed windows on both levels of the house catch the breezes blowing in off the lake. Three tall brick chimneys perch atop the roof, and the two closest to each end of the house have long, narrow cylindrical flues extending above.

Every effort has been made to return this station to its 1920s appearance. And it's very evident that much work and love has gone into the beautiful landscaping here, especially considering this is such an isolated outpost. The charming grounds include several flower beds bordered in stone and filled with a bright mixture of annuals. Beautiful roses and beds of lilies brighten up the front yard, while bordering one side yard are wild roses, their thick, pink frills dotting the dark-green bushes. A large section of the back yard has been cultivated into a vegetable garden, bordered by thick grape vines wrapping around their supporting posts and connecting wires.

During the summer months you can take a guided tour of the tower and the

keeper's house, which now includes a museum. As an additional bonus, a park ranger greets visitors in the 1920s' guise — including lighthouse keeper's uniform — of Herbert "Toots" Winfield, an assistant lightkeeper here in 1923. This living-history presentation includes colorful stories about the lighthouse and the people who once called it home. Because of the dedication of many park employees, Raspberry Island is one of the few places where you can actually see what an active turn-of-the-century lighthouse must have been like, right down to socks hanging on the clothesline.

And as you leave, look up to the tower's walkway for a final memory of this spectacular station — lightkeeper "Winfield," who has climbed there to wave good-bye.

Outer Island Lighthouse

"The red clay banks of Outer Island spill down into the turquoise water of Lake Superior, leaving only a narrow strip of beach to catch the driftwood washed ashore."

The red clay banks of Outer Island spill down into the turquoise water of Lake Superior, leaving only a narrow strip of beach to catch the driftwood washed ashore. In several places, trees have overrun the banks to encroach nearly to the water's edge.

This northernmost of the Apostle Islands became home to a beautiful lighthouse in 1874. Poking out from shore in front of the lighthouse complex is a cement pier that provides access, but boulders near the dock make the approach hazardous. After docking, you must conquer the lengthy flight of steps that climb between tram rails 100 feet to the top of the banks. The heavy clay is terraced near the tramway to provide more stability, and large boulders have been scattered along the shore to prevent erosion.

The three-story keeper's dwelling is constructed of reddish-brown brick. Rows of 12-paned windows with arched white trim line the first two levels, plus third-story dormer windows poke out from either side of the roof. A huge chimney dominates the tapered roofline at the back of the house, and the sloping roof of the kitchen, attached to the south side, begins just under the second-story windows there.

A small, white wood passageway connects the house to the tower, which rises 90 feet. Only a few small, square windows break the smoothness of its white brick, except near the top, where a black band sets off a row of arched windows just below a circular walkway. The walkway — supported by decorative arches and surrounded by a black metal railing — encircles a small, round, white room with a doorway providing access to the lantern room above. A smaller walkway and railing surrounding the 10-sided lantern room was used by keepers to clean the outside of the glass panes. A black ventilator ball caps the room, now missing its third-order Fresnel lens, which was removed when the light was automated in 1961. Part of the light's clockwork mechanism, however, remains.

Surrounding the light is a lush lawn, with several large mountain ash and lilac bushes poking up from the smooth, green carpet. Behind one of the trees is a square, red fuel building, with a cracked, unused sidewalk running from it to meet the house. Farther away, the white wood whistle house nestles close to the edge of the hill, its air compressor still inside. But the twin fog horns extending from the cupola are no longer used to warn ships away from the dangerous waters off Outer Island.

OUTER ISLAND LIGHTHOUSE

Devils Island Lighthouse

"Native Americans called it the Island of Evil Spirits because of the eerie howling echoes that emanated from the caves when waves struck them."

Belying its name, Devils Island is one of the most beautiful of all the Apostle Islands. From a distance the powerful shoreline in front of the lighthouse appears to be an unbroken, 40-foot-high wall of sandstone, its red layers streaked with deep-gray and white to create a rich tapestry. But also composing the forbidding shoreline is a puzzle of small caves, hidden coves, and tumbled shelves of stone thrown unceremoniously down into the blue depths of Lake Superior. The submerged rocks and dangerous waterline caves serve to isolate the island by making it almost unapproachable. And it was the caves that gave the island its name. Native Americans called it the Island of Evil Spirits because of the eerie howling echoes that emanated from the caves when waves struck them.

Lightkeepers and their families probably considered this remote rock an uninviting assignment, but it did have one plus — regular visits by beautiful hawks.

This large station required two houses — a keeper's house built in 1891 and an assistant keeper's home constructed five years later. They are nearly identical in their strong, stunning architecture. Each is a sprawling two stories, with red brick walls and a sharply angled gray roof reaching down to protect the front porch. The keeper's house, nearest shore, has a beautiful brick arch framing the porch, with a delicate, oval window still illuminating the interior. The assistant's dwelling has less-impressive, plain, white support posts for the porch corners, and the oval window is absent.

The grounds surrounding the houses and running 300 yards northwest up the shore to the light tower were once cleared. But without constant human presence, bushes and small trees have taken a foothold, making it necessary for park personnel to remove the encroaching vegetation every few years. A few older pines poke above the island's treeline, but none can compete with the 82-foot-high white steel tower. A wide metal cylinder — supported by thin, slightly curved braces — rises to meet a slightly wider, circular room below the lantern room. A few round windows peer out from just beneath the walkway surrounding the lantern room, and the red roof and ventilator ball topped with a weathervane provide the only bright color on the island.

The first tower here — its beacon lit in 1891 — was a temporary wood structure. Ten years later it was replaced by the tower still standing today and fitted with a third-order Fresnel lens. In 1989 that lens — even though an acrylic light outside the lantern room had been and still was used — was carefully removed, cleaned and refurbished. The delicate job took three years, and finally in 1992 the Devils Island guiding light returned home. Though still no longer lit, it can be clearly seen through the lantern room's crosshatched glass panes from just off-shore.

About 200 yards farther west along the rugged shoreline, a white steel-skeleton radio tower stretches skyward.

DEVILS ISLAND LIGHTHOUSE

Sand Island Lighthouse

" The keeper's house and tower are the only structures of their kind in the Apostles made from native stone. "

The shoreline of Sand Island is bordered with a jumbled mass of deep, brown stone, with the level lawn of the lighthouse complex resting atop the underlying bedrock and creating a shelf 10 feet above the water line. The keeper's house and tower are constructed of the brown rock, making them the only structures of their kind in the Apostles made from native stone, and their rich color blends beautifully with the hardwood forest behind. The smoothly shaped stone of the two-story keeper's house, built in 1881, is formed into arches above the doorway, and the 12-paned windows are framed by dark-green shutters to protect against the varied weather of Lake Superior. The gently sloping red metal roof is trimmed with decorative supports beneath the white eaves plus a white cross beam and spire at the gables.

The distinctive light tower dominates the northwest corner of the house. The base is square, with large buttresses at each corner for support. A second set of supports are above the first, and above them the square tower becomes circular. A black metal walkway and railing surround the 10-sided lantern room, which still houses a modern white beacon that was automated in 1921. An oil house and privy, both made of red brick with red roofs to match the main house, sit at the back of the clearing. At the shoreline a wood stairway leads down to the wave-swept rocks and a small landing area.

Tour boats drop off visitors two miles from the light, but it's an easy walk along the trail leading through a section of virgin white pine to the lighthouse on the north end of the island. Volunteer lightkeepers offer guided tours from mid-June to Labor Day.

SAND ISLAND LIGHTHOUSE

Wisconsin Point Light

" Together the twins make up the world's largest freshwater sand bar. "

Wisconsin Point is a thin strip of land stretching up from the south to nearly meet a similar strip of land — Minnesota Point — coming down from the north. Together these twins, which protect the harbor of Superior, Wisconsin, make up the world's largest freshwater sand bar.

Poking into Lake Superior from Wisconsin Point is a smooth cement pier, and at its end the lighthouse (also known as the Superior Entry South Breakwater light) rests on a 10-foot-high foundation with a metal railing around the edge and a wide cement stairway dropping down to the pier. The design of the white concrete house is unusual — an oval shape with the vertical ribs of the metal roof sweeping around the curves like a pleated skirt. Black doorways and rectangular windows mark the sides of the two-story structure, and a small chimney looks out over the peak of the roof.

The round, white cement tower — with rows of round porthole windows illuminating its interior — rises from the northeast end of the house. At the parapet a decorative black metal railing surrounds the lantern room, which is glazed in distinctive cross-hatched panes and covered with a red metal cap and ventilator ball. From the walkway a short antenna stretches skyward.

Offshore near downtown Superior is Barker's Island, with shops, a marina, a children's playground and a maritime museum aboard the world's only whale-back freighter still in existence — the S.S. *Meteor*, which was first launched here in 1896. Guided tours of the ship are conducted May through September. For a current schedule, call (715) 392-5742. Boat tours of the harbor also leave from Barker's Island and include a trip under Duluth's aerial lift bridge. Call (218)

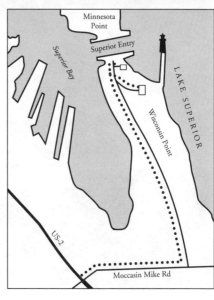

DIRECTIONS: At the intersection of US-2 and Moccasin Mike Rd. on the southeast edge of Superior (US-2 changes from regular highway to freeway at this intersection), turn northeast onto Moccasin Mike Rd. and go about 1.4 miles to an unmarked blacktop road. (A sign on the right just before the junction points the way left to the Wisconsin Point Beach and lighthouse.) Turn left (north) onto the unnamed road and drive approximately 3.3 miles to another unnamed road, just before a stop sign. Turn right (east) and follow that road about 0.1 mile to a parking area near the breakwater and look for the light on the end of the breakwater.

For a different and closer perspective, return to the main road, turn left (south), go about 150 feet, turn left (east) onto the gravel road and follow it about 0.2 mile to another parking area near the breakwater. You can view the light from shore or walk out onto the breakwater for a closer look.

Duluth Harbor North Pier Light

" You can view freighters coming into the canal from all parts of the world."

Along the shoreline of Duluth, Minnesota, a canal was dug as a shortcut from Lake Superior to the harbor at Superior Bay, and the entrance to this canal was bordered by both the North and South Breakwaters and their lights.

The pier reaching out to Duluth's North Breakwater light is a substantial waterfront landmark. The smooth concrete sides are reinforced near the water's edge with metal sheathing, while overhead, huge lights banish even the darkest nights. The foundation surrounding the light tower has also been vastly improved. A thick concrete wall surrounds the light's platform, which angles down sharply to meet a row of black metal reinforcement that touches the water. Rising up from that sturdy foundation is the smooth, white circular tower. A black band wraps its base, including the doorway, and farther upward the whiteness is broken only by an occasional square, black window. The circular walkway near the top is bordered with a black iron railing, and the black lantern room and cap protect the white beacon that still guides travelers into the waters of Duluth.

Only yards away from the light in Canal Park, you can also view the two south breakwater lights plus freighters coming into the canal from all parts of the world. Benches line the grassy park, and exhibits at the Canal Park Marine Museum include ships' models, a replica of a ship's cabin and pilot house, and a

"Stretching back from shore, the city of Duluth climbs a series of beautiful, rolling hills."

Coast Guard surfboat on display just outside. Nearby, a gigantic floating museum — the bulk carrier *William A. Irving* — is open for guided tours that include close-up looks at its charming staterooms and four-story engine rooms.

At the west edge of the park, the canal is bisected by a towering lift bridge, which on busy days is called upon often to allow passage to boats. Tours of the harbor, offered during the summer months, depart from the convention center dock near the lift bridge.

Stretching back from shore behind Canal Park, the city of Duluth climbs a series of beautiful, rolling hills.

DIRECTIONS: From I-35 in Duluth, take exit 256-B (Lake Ave. and 5th Ave. West) to Lake Ave. (If you are coming from the south, you will go about 0.4 mile on a service road before reaching Lake Ave., where a sign points right, to Canal Park Dr.) Turn east onto Lake Ave. and go about 0.1 mile, toward Lake Superior and the lift bridge, to the traffic signal at the bottom of the hill. Stay in the left lane and continue straight ahead on Canal Park Dr. about 0.4 mile to the parking areas near the canal. As you walk to the canal, look for the North Breakwater light and the South Breakwater Outer light to the left and the South Breakwater Inner light to the right, across the canal.

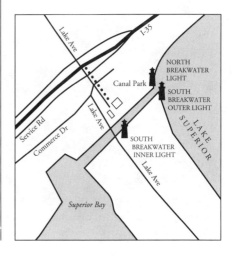

Duluth Harbor South Breakwater Outer Light

The massive pier extending from the southern of two breakwaters marking the entrance to a canal into Duluth Harbor is a poured concrete structure complete with overhead lighting. The foundation for the light tower at the end of the pier is an even more impressive structure, with long, sloping sides dipping into the water and a wide flight of stairs running up to the front door of the light.

The two-story house is white brick topped with a red metal roof. Several narrow, arched, black-trimmed windows rest on heavy stone sills.

Rising from the southeastern corner of the building is the square, white brick tower, with arched windows and thick, black trim peeking out just above the roofline of the house. Above the windows, a wide walkway is bordered by a metal railing, and the beautiful green, diamond-shaped panes of glass create a cross-hatched pattern as they encircle the lantern. Covering the tower is a red metal roof matching the shiny roof of the dwelling below.

(DIRECTIONS and map, page 73.)

Duluth Harbor South Breakwater Inner Light

The inner light of the South Breakwater in Duluth is a black cylinder supported by four metal legs and a network of trusses. A round, white room balances at the top, with a black metal railing surrounding the walkway outside. Above this room the octagonal lantern room has its own walkway and railing, and a black metal cap and ventilator ball protect the beacon within.

The base of the tower rests at the beginning of the breakwater, hidden behind a curtain of dark-green foliage from lilacs that have flourished here.

(DIRECTIONS and map, page 73.)

" The base of the tower is hidden behind a curtain of dark-green foliage from lilacs that have flourished here. "

DULUTH LIFT BRIDGE

Minnesota Point Lighthouse Ruins

Minnesota Point is a beautiful strip of land stretching south out into Lake Superior. It is covered with a mixture of towering pines, grassy wildflower meadows, and sandy shoreline, all of which attract a variety of wildlife, including black bears. The walk out to the light — a mile on a hard-packed dirt path followed by a half mile of slightly harder treading over a sandy trail — leads through the most beautiful areas of the point.

The remains of the light are centered in a clearing, with only a few small trees rising to compete with the old tower. The long-forgotten red brick structure is a deteriorating shell, its lantern long since disappeared and its walls beginning to crumble near the top. Square, black emptiness is all that remains of the doorway, once securely latched by a keeper as he made his daily rounds.

When this light was built in 1858, the light tower was close to the water's edge. Years of shifting sands have changed the shape of the point, however, and so the tower now stands about two blocks from shore.

DIRECTIONS: From I-35 in Duluth, take exit 256-B (Lake Ave. and 5th Ave. West) to Lake Ave. (If you are coming from the south, you will go about 0.4 mile on a service road before reaching Lake Ave., where a sign points right, to Canal Park Dr.) Turn east onto Lake Ave. and go about 0.1 mile, toward Lake Superior and the lift bridge, to the traffic signal at the bottom of the hill. Continue following Lake Ave. by turning right (south), going one block, turning left (east), and then heading directly over the lift bridge approximately 4.8 miles to the road's end at the airport. (Lake Ave. changes to Minnesota Ave. along this stretch.)

Park in marked areas on the roadside just before the airport. The trail to the light begins behind the first airport building and is marked by a gate erected to keep cars off from the road. From the gate, follow the trail until you are about 2 blocks past the end of the runway. At this point the road turns left to a pumping station; the route to the light continues straight ahead on a two-track. The two-track leads ¼ mile (past a white cabin on the right) to a steel tower. Pass to the left of the tower and, following one of the trails along the Lake Superior shore, walk another ¼ mile to the light, in a large, open area in the middle of a sand bar.

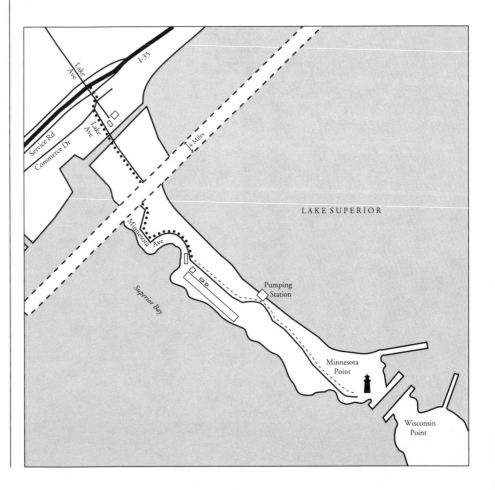

MINNESOTA POINT LIGHTHOUSE RUINS

Two Harbors Lighthouse Museum

"The huge square tower is similar to a castle's keep."

Iron Ore played a large part in the development of many Lake Superior communities. The first ship to depart Two Harbors with its holds filled with ore left in 1884. Over the next eight years, this sleepy, little town turned into one of the busiest ports on the lake. A lighthouse became essential and was built in 1892.

Today, the Two Harbors lightstation is an interesting mix of exhibits illuminating our maritime heritage, but the crowning glory is the remarkable lighthouse and tower. The spacious two-story brick house is painted a subdued red, with its plentiful rectangular windows all trimmed in white, including the smaller attic windows beneath each gable. Nearby is a second, smaller house, built to provide more space for the additional keepers assigned here as the busy station grew.

Dominating the southwest corner of the main house and rising about 50 feet is the huge, square tower, which is similar to a castle's keep, right down to the buttresses supporting the base. Three sets of double windows bring in plenty of light, and graceful brickwork arches around small, round windows just below the walkway. A decorative metal railing surrounds the square walkway, and the octagonal lantern room houses two airport beacons, still working, which replaced the original fourth-order Fresnel lens in 1970. Just east of the tower, a small recess encloses and protects the dwelling's front door.

In front of the lighthouse, a beautiful fog whistle building sits closer to the edge of the bluff overlooking Lake Superior. The white, wooden one-story building is shingled in dark red, and a small, square room rises from the roofline to support two black fog horns pointing out toward the lake.

The building has been turned into a museum housing fishing displays and photos from the 19th and early 20th centuries. The newest pilot house off the freighter *Frontenac* is also on display, providing an excellent opportunity to see first-hand some of the inner workings of a freighter. (An older pilot house off the same ship is on display at the Fairport Harbor Lighthouse Museum in Ohio.)

Although the light was automated in 1981, Coast Guard personnel used the station until 1987, when it was turned over to the Lake County Historical Society. The group's members are restoring the tower and house, plus several other buildings dotting the complex. They also run the museum and conduct tours of the light for a small admission fee.

The lighthouse and museum are open 9:30 a.m. to 6:00 p.m. Sunday through Thursday, and 9:30 a.m. to 8:00 p.m. Friday and Saturday. For more information, including tour schedules, write Lake County Historical Society, P.O. Box 313, Two Harbors, MN 55616, or phone (218) 834-4898.

(DIRECTIONS and map, page 80.)

FRONTENAC PILOT HOUSE

TWO HARBORS LIGHTHOUSE MUSEUM

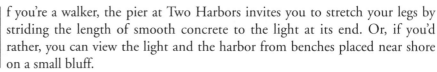

Two Harbors East Breakwater Light

If you're a walker, the pier at Two Harbors invites you to stretch your legs by striding the length of smooth concrete to the light at its end. Or, if you'd rather, you can view the light and the harbor from benches placed near shore on a small bluff.

The 25-foot-high steel tower is supported at its base by four steel legs, creating an open bottom half. The second level is an enclosed room with a stairway leading from the pier up to a doorway. Atop the structure is a walkway and an octagonal lantern room protecting a small, modern beacon that still shines over the deep blue Lake Superior waters.

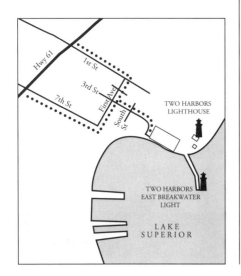

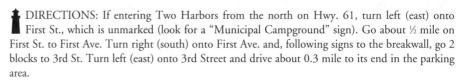

DIRECTIONS: If entering Two Harbors from the north on Hwy. 61, turn left (east) onto First St., which is unmarked (look for a "Municipal Campground" sign). Go about ½ mile on First St. to First Ave. Turn right (south) onto First Ave. and, following signs to the breakwall, go 2 blocks to 3rd St. Turn left (east) onto 3rd Street and drive about 0.3 mile to its end in the parking area.

If entering Two Harbors from the south on Hwy. 61, turn right (east) at the traffic signal on 7th St. and go ½ mile to First Ave. Turn left (north) onto First Ave. and, following the signs to the breakwall, drive about 0.3 mile to 3rd St. Turn right (east) onto 3rd St. and go about 0.3 mile to its end in the parking area.

The Two Harbors lighthouse is at the northeast end of the parking area, and the Pierhead light is on the end of the breakwall, southeast of the parking area.

SPLIT ROCK LIGHTHOUSE

Split Rock Lighthouse Museum

"Each explosion showered workers with dislodged rock and other debris."

Split Rock lighthouse is one of the most recognizable lighthouses on the Great Lakes, both because of its location and the beauty that resulted from the craftsmanship that went into its construction. It sits near the edge of a huge rock bluff that dramatically plunges nearly 170 feet to Lake Superior. The rock face is a mixture of deep grays and streaks of white, with patches of gold splashed across the rock closer to the waterline. A fringe of green has gained a foothold at the crest of the bluff and surrounds the lighthouse, while south of the light, bushes and small birch spill down slightly less steep rock to the lake below.

A light here was deemed necessary to warn ships of the dangerous magnetic properties of the local rock, which threw off compasses, with sometimes dire results.

Construction, which began in 1909, was a challenge. Materials had to be brought to the then-isolated site by boat and hoisted up the steep cliff by derrick, which could only be used at the whim of the weather. If it were too windy, for instance, nothing could be lifted. Building the foundations of the tower and house required blasting through solid bedrock, and each explosion showered workers with dislodged rock and other debris, fortunately with no serious injury. And the rugged workmen had to sleep in tents, which they often had to hold down during storms to keep their only shelter from blowing away.

The lighthouse was completed in 1910, and when its third-order Fresnel lens was lit, it could sometimes be seen as far away as the Apostle Islands, 45 miles to the south. It was standard procedure at most lights to count the revolutions of the beacon, and the first keeper here, Orren P. (Pete) Young, would sit in a kitchen rocker and watch his lantern's revolving light as it flashed against the chimney outside. He could quickly tell if the revolving mechanism was slowing down and would leave to adjust it if necessary, sometimes tying a rope around his waist to keep from being blown over the cliff during violent storms.

For the first six years, the keepers here received all supplies by way of the derrick used by the construction crews. In 1916 an elevated tramway was built, which made it much easier to bring goods ashore, and finally in 1934 the station acquired a truck.

The 45-foot-tall light tower is built on a curved rise of stone where the soft carpet of lawn stops abruptly only feet from the bluff's edge. A white, octagonal cement foundation, topped with its own decorative border, supports the eight-sided tower, constructed of pale gold bricks. As the gold tower rises, it narrows slightly, and on each side a rectangular window, with a black overhang and trim, peers out over the lake. A second narrow, decorative white stone border bisects the tower, and the gold brick walls above are broken only by a few small windows with heavy, white lintels. A narrow, black walkway circles the tower just below the large lantern room, which is glazed with dozens of panes of glass on the front half and sheathed in black metal at the back. A ladder provides precarious access to the roof, which is circled by a small hand rail.

" The keeper would sit in a kitchen rocker and watch his lantern's revolving light as it flashed against the chimney outside. He would leave to adjust the light if necessary, sometimes tying a rope around his waist to keep from being blown over the cliff during violent storms. "

Each November 10, the third-order clam-shell Fresnel lens inside shines in memory of the sailors who lost their lives during the sinking of the *Edmund Fitzgerald*. Though that is the only scheduled lighting, the park manager, with Coast Guard approval, does switch on the beacon at a few other times.

Attached to the rear of the light tower is a square, flat-topped single-story building made of a slightly paler gold brick above a square, white foundation. Decorative carved stone dividers climb the walls between each of the many square windows. A stone border similar to that of the tower runs along the top of

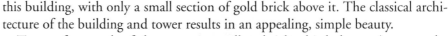

this building, with only a small section of gold brick above it. The classical architecture of the building and tower results in an appealing, simple beauty.

Twenty feet north of the tower is a yellow brick whistle house (open to the public), its huge horns stretching toward the lake from the dark red roofline. Though a useful warning device, the foghorn didn't always work as intended. Fog can distort sound, and so depending on conditions, the horn could sound much closer or much farther away than it actually was. In some instances a ship would sail too close to the horn and the sound would pass overhead unheard.

During one such incident in the 1930s, a lightkeeper named Covell realized that a ship was having difficulty hearing the fog signal and had approached too close to the dangerous rocks near shore. Covell dashed down the steep hill to the dock and blew as loudly as he could on a hand whistle to signal the ship that it was in great peril. Just in time, a crew member heard the whistle and the pilot was able to turn the ship away from potential tragedy.

This light was in operation until 1969. Today, some buildings are fenced off, including three unique two-story garages. The first level of each is cream-colored, the second story is dark red, and each is illuminated by several 12-paned windows and topped with a cupola.

Directly in front of the garages are a trio of square two-story houses that served as dwellings to the many keepers assigned here. The tan brick structures have identical front entryways, plus wide red-shingled overhangs with heavy arched supports attached to the backs. And the roofs of these homes were designed to collect rainwater, which the families who lived here held in basement cisterns until used. Today, one of the houses is home to the light station's site manager. Another is open to visitors and is furnished with many pre-1924 pieces, including a wood stove still occasionally used to bake bread.

In 1971 the lighthouse buildings and 2,000 surrounding acres were designated a state park. Today, the lighthouse complex is a Minnesota Historic Site that is administered by the Minnesota Historical Society. The group also added a History Center building, which houses exhibits, a film on the history of this lightstation, and a gift shop. You can also take a guided tour of the tower and fog whistle building, both of which have been restored to their 1920s appearance. And by following the old pathway south of the complex down to what was once the base of the tramway, you can walk down to the water's edge, where you can take excellent photos of this light.

There is an admission fee to enter the lighthouse complex. A separate vehicle pass is required for entrance to the other sections of Split Rock Lighthouse State Park. Facilities there include 12 miles of hiking trails maintained year round, a cart-in campground with shower building, backpack campsites, and a large picnic area with two shelters. The state park, including the lighthouse complex, is open May 15 to October 15, 9 a.m. to 5 p.m. daily. From October 16 to May 14, only the history center is open, 12 to 4 p.m. Friday through Sunday. For more information, contact Split Rock Lighthouse, 2010 Highway 61 East, Two Harbors, Minnesota 55616; (218) 226-4372.

DIRECTIONS: Split Rock lighthouse is located in Split Rock State Park, approximately 19.2 miles North of Two Harbors and about 4.9 miles South of Beaver Bay on Hwy 61. Turn east into the state park, which is well-marked, and go about 0.1 mile to the office, on the right. You can pick up a map of the area here and then continue on the road left to the welcome center and lighthouse parking area.

Grand Marais Light

The light that marks the harbor of Grand Marais is a 35-foot-tall, white steel structure supported by four legs. A ladder leads up to the watchroom, a small, enclosed area topped by short, decorative posts that support a round walkway. The octagonal lantern room, capped in red, holds an operational beacon.

The old keeper's house, in downtown Grand Marais, houses a maritime museum with historical and nautical exhibits from the Grand Marais area. The museum is open during the summer months from 10 a.m. to 5 p.m. weekdays and 12 to 5 p.m. on Sundays.

DIRECTIONS: If traveling north on Hwy. 61 into Grand Marais, go to the bottom of a hill, and as you approach the business district, turn right (east) onto Wisconsin St. If traveling south into Grand Marais on Hwy. 61, turn left (east) onto West 2nd Ave. as you near the downtown area, and go one block to Wisconsin St. Turn right (west) onto Wisconsin. Park anywhere along Wisconsin and look for the light out in the harbor to the south, at the end of the breakwall.

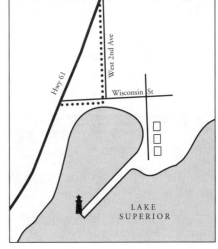

Thunder Bay Main Lighthouse

Thunder Bay — a showcase of Lake Superior beauty and the world's largest grain port — has long been an area busy and essential enough to warrant a lighthouse. The first lighthouse here was built at the mouth of the Kaministikwia River during the 1800s, when the area was known as Fort William.

Problems popped up quickly. The lighthouse complex, which included two range lights, was built in a low-lying area of the river delta, and the walkways were regularly ripped apart by winter ice or floated away during periods of high water. And mist, which rose from the rivermouth each night and stayed well into the morning, obscured the lights, a serious problem that necessitated both ranges being increased 10 feet in height. But halfway into the project in 1895, workmen stopped when they realized that if they continued the angle of the new walls upward 10 feet, the lightkeeper would have only a 10-inch-square space in which to stand and light the lamp. Design corrections were made, and the height increase was completed.

Later, a series of immense four-mile-long rough stone breakwaters were thrust out into the waters of majestic Thunder Bay. In 1937 the lighthouse that stands today was built at the end of the southernmost breakwater on a very unusual foundation. Two long, narrow cement strips rest beneath the house's two side edges. Each corner of each 2-foot-thick strip is built up to form a 4-foot-high pyramid that supports a corner of the lighthouse. Tucked in the middle of the resulting 6-foot-high open space beneath the structure is a 4- by 6-foot storage room, with its own bright red door and trim. A gray metal stairway runs from a wooden platform resting just above the water level up to the entrance to the main building.

That 20-foot square, 31-foot-tall, white wooden dwelling is trimmed and accented in red — on each corner, around the doorway, and even diesel motor exhaust and intake vents poking out of the first-story walls. Several of the square, red-trimmed windows on the second level have been boarded up. From the center of the reddish-brown roof, the square tower rises only an additional five feet to the walkway and red metal railing surrounding the octagonal lantern room. Inside is an operational modern beacon. Gold lichen clings to the dark stones surrounding the lighthouse, which is reflected in a blur of white across the surface of the dark blue water.

Breaking the rougher waters of Lake Superior is the distant outline of an unusually shaped peninsula. Ojibwa legend tells of a time when the Great Spirit showed them a rich vein of silver, admonishing them to never reveal its location to the Europeans, lest the Great Spirit be turned to stone. Predictably, some unfortunate soul couldn't keep the secret, and as a result, perished and also caused the Great Spirit to turn into the peninsula now known as the "Sleeping Giant."

Other islands dot the waters of Thunder Bay, and its rugged shoreline gives way to a thick curtain of deep green where pine forests sweep across the land. Overlooking the wide bay, majestic Mt. McKay rises hundreds of feet towards

THUNDER BAY MAIN LIGHTHOUSE

"Halfway into the project, workmen realized that if they continued the angle of the new walls upward 10 feet, the lightkeeper would have only a 10-inch-square space in which to stand and light the lamp."

the sky.

Standing on a smaller hill east of town on Highway 17A is a monument to Terry Fox, a once-unknown Canadian runner who refused to give in to cancer. After losing a leg to the disease in 1977 at age 19, Fox began the "Marathon of Hope," a run that was to take him across Canada to raise funds for cancer research. His courage galvanized a nation, and his countrymen's hearts were with him when he was forced to give up his run near Thunder Bay. As a symbol of his nation's love, the beautiful monument here (as well as one in Ottawa, Canada's capitol city) was built after cancer finally claimed Fox at 22 years of age. It is a stunning location to visit.

On the outskirts of town is another popular destination, Old Fort William, a reconstructed fur trading post. Covered entryways supported by huge tree trunks lead into a huge, modern interpretive building. Inside, the powerful theme is repeated in expansive murals and displays, and outside you can explore the fort's more than 40 historic buildings plus a huge wharf and canoe landing on the Kaministikwia River. Guides are ready to not only explain minute details of what life was like for fur traders long ago but also show you. Dressed in period costumes, they invite you to join as they bring furs from Indian campsites up to the fort's store. You can also experience the culinary treats of centuries past by partaking in a delicious lunch — complete with warm, fresh-baked bread — served daily. In this fascinating environment, you become a part of history and history becomes a part of you.

If you're looking for a more tangible souvenir, try the nearby amethyst mine, where you can mine the gems yourself. Only seven countries in the world can boast amethyst mines, and Thunder Bay is in the middle of Canada's amethyst country.

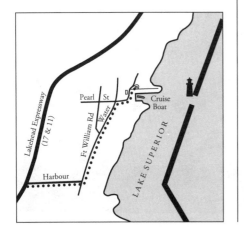

DIRECTIONS: The best way to view this offshore light close up is during a two-hour cruise aboard the *Welcome Cruiseship*, which departs daily from the Thunder Bay North Marina Dock.

To get there, from Hwy. 11/Hwy.17 (Lakehead Expressway) in Thunder Bay, turn east onto the Harbour Expressway and go approximately 2.1 miles (3.4 km.) to Fort William Rd. Turn left (north) onto Fort William and go about 2.1 miles (3.4 km.) to where Fort William Rd. jogs left. Continue straight ahead on Water St. about 0.9 mile (1.4 km.) to Pearl St. (Look for a Thunder Bay Fire Station, on the left at this intersection.) Turn right (east) onto Pearl, cross over the railroad tracks and, following the road to the left, continue another 0.2 mile (0.3 km.) to the Harbour Cruise ticket office, in an old ship's pilot house, on the right, just past the old Canadian National Railway depot.

The cruise ship operates from May 29 to early October. Also available is a cruise that runs from the harbor up the river to Fort William. For further information contact Welcomeship Ltd., Box 89, Vickers Heights, Ontario P0T 2Z0; (807) 683-8849.

Trowbridge Island Lighthouse

The inhospitable shoreline of Trowbridge Island, 15 miles east of Thunder Bay, guards one of the loveliest lightstations we've seen. Edging the small island are steep, nearly unclimbable 15-foot-high cliffs — a barren mass of lichen-covered rock with a dark band of wetness near the water's edge and an orange line skirting along above it. Back from the cliff's edges, the small island rises in a rounded heap covered with a thick carpet of pines. The only break in the forest's dark green is the winding red-and-white wooden stairway

"Towering purple cliffs create a natural backdrop that would put any artist to shame."

that climbs to the light tower at the island's center.

Perched at that "peak," is the wooden 25-foot-tall tower, interrupted by a few rectangular windows and topped with a bright red lantern room that contrasts with the muted colors of the trees below. Still inside is the beautiful Fresnel lens that once guided ships around the treacherous surrounding islands and into Thunder Bay. Each of the glass panes on the room's ten sides claims a different, beautiful view of Lake Superior. To the northeast, the towering purple cliffs of the peninsula known as "The Sleeping Giant" create a natural backdrop that would put any artist to shame, its rippled rock cliffs stretching far above the sapphire waves to reach for the clouds.

The crisp whiteness of the tower is mirrored in the nearby keeper's house. A beautiful porch stretches along the entire front of the dwelling, ready to take advantage of lake breezes that almost continually sweep in. The porch railing is set in a starburst pattern along each panel, and decorative trim near the roofline adds to the delicate charm. The second-story windows peer out just above the dark red roofline to form unusual "half-dormers."

To build this lighthouse, a small docking area was constructed below the sheer cliff wall, and materials hoisted up via a derrick secured to a cement foundation on top of the rock overhead. Added later and still standing close to shore is a second docking area, a red-roofed, white wooden building standing on a huge cement foundation that angles sharply down to the water. A stairway climbs up the side of the foundation to the building. Nearby are two sheds erected to provide protection for the various machinery and apparatus, including the foghorn mechanism that was necessary to run this light station.

Despite these "civilized" touches, however, Trowbridge Island remains a small piece of wilderness, nearly unchanged.

"Still inside is the beautiful Fresnel lens that once guided ships around the treacherous surrounding islands and into Thunder Bay."

Point Porphyry Lighthouse

As shipping traffic increased on northern Lake Superior, the many area islands created great hazards, including the strange magnetic properties of their rock, which could wreak havoc with a compass, thus pulling a ship dangerously off course. The lighthouse on Point Porphyry helped mariners evade these dangers and make it safely home.

Point Porphyry is a flat expanse of dark gray stone, covered with a thick carpet of pines and hardwoods, that reaches out into Lake Superior like an arrowhead at the southern tip of Edward Island, 30 miles east of Thunder Bay. Curving gracefully around this island is a chain of smaller islands, appearing to float in the dark turquoise of Lake Superior.

A patch of forest was cleared on Point Porphyry, and in 1873 a lighthouse was established there. The 48-foot-tall tower is a wide, white metal cylinder. A small room off its base provides access, and four skeletal supports reach down from the red metal walkway to provide stability. The white lantern room houses a beacon that still warns of the dangerous shoreline below. Two large, white keeper's dwellings are tucked into the deep green forest behind the light, while closer to shore, a white fog horn building with red roof provides a bright spot of color in the otherwise subdued landscape.

Although isolated, Edward Island at least once was the center of maritime action. In 1929 the laker *Thordoc* ran aground in shallow waters off the point. The only way to raise and free the ship was to lighten its load, which happened to be flour. The crew threw hundreds of bags overboard, much to the delight of local residents, who were able to retrieve them and use the contents.

> " *The strange magnetic properties of the rock could wreak havoc with a compass, thus pulling a ship dangerously off course.* "

Shaganash Light

The Shaganash light actually sits west of Shaganash Island on a tiny island with the uninspiring name #10. Waves crash against the black rocks tumbled along the rugged shore, spraying across the few bushes and grasses growing on the cleared patch of land that holds the light.

The square, 24-foot-tall tower, built close to shore in 1910, is capped by a bright red walkway and lantern room and still warns ships of the hazardous travel over this part of the lake.

Battle Island Lighthouse

The first lightstation on Battle Island was established in 1877. The tower that stands today was built in 1911 and overlooks the island's shore from a high, rounded bluff of black rock, its crevices and ledges sprinkled with deep-gold lichen, its base washed by the thundering waves of Lake Superior. The entire island — seven miles south of Rossport, Ontario — is a naturalist's paradise, from the black gravel beaches, with rocky sentinels standing offshore, to the thick perfume of the pine forest covering its interior.

As we approached the light, a thick fog that had persisted all morning slowly moved aside to expose the poured concrete walls of the 43-foot-high, octagonal, white tower. Only a few rectangular windows look out over the expanse of deep, blue water 75 feet below. The bright red, octagonal metal walkway and lantern room still protect the beacon burning within and provide a colorful contrast to the surrounding subdued beauty.

The quiet scene is deceptive, though, and can be transformed into raging fury when struck by the full force of a Lake Superior storm. Gale force winds during a 1977 blow, for instance, sent spray from the wild surf up the 75-foot cliff plus another 45 feet to cover the light tower. And before the storm was spent, it had blown the windows out of the lantern room.

The beautiful two-story keeper's house rests near the light in a small area cleared from the surrounding pines and mountain ash. The dwelling was home to both the head keeper and an assistant, and like modern duplexes the house is a mirror of itself. Two porches, with a small enclosed room separating them, stretch along the front of the house and are covered by a reddish-brown roof supported by bright red posts. Two sets of gray wood steps reach down to the small

" Gale force winds during a 1977 blow sent spray from the wild surf up the 75-foot cliff plus another 45 feet to cover the light tower. "

"The tower overlooks the island's shore from a high, rounded bluff of black rock."

BERT SAASTO, THE LAST LIGHTKEEPER ON THE GREAT LAKES.

surrounding lawn, with patches of black rock rising up from the green.

Beautiful six-paned windows look out from beneath the red-shingled roof, which has tapered gables, bright red trim running along the eaves, and twin chimneys rising above the peak. Two slender trees spread their branches across the front of the house, partially hiding the second story. A small red and white outbuilding brushes up against the forest at the edge of the clearing. And a ribbon of concrete walkway is draped over the black rock from the house down to the dock area.

We were given a tour of this light by Albert "Bert" Saasto, the present caretaker of Battle Island. Bert was assistant lightkeeper here, and when he left this post in 1991, he did so as the last lightkeeper on the Great Lakes.

Slate Islands Lighthouse

The Slate Islands spread a protective arm around the northern shoreline of much larger Patterson Island, which is home to the Slate Islands light. The Patterson Island shoreline varies from gravelly beaches to steep slopes that plunge dramatically into the emerald green of the lake. Small bushes

" The light tower surveys its domain from a clearing at the crest of the island's highest point."

"More than 500 caribou are scattered throughout the heavily wooded island."

dot the face of the cliffs down to the water's edge, and patches of white lichen spread over the rocky surface. Twenty-five feet above, the vertical line of the rock is continued in the slender trunks of pines perched precariously at the summit. More than 500 caribou are scattered throughout the heavily wooded nine-square-mile island, which is a game sanctuary.

Near a narrow cement dock, the keeper's house claims a sand and gravel beach as its front lawn. The white two-story house is trimmed in red and protected by a reddish-brown roof. The dark green limbs of nearby pines reach out toward the dwelling, and the hills behind are carpeted with the moss-covered pines and hardwoods. Beyond a hill to the south of the keeper's house, an area was cleared to provide space for other buildings. Another two-story dwelling there, complete with two cupolas at its peak, matches the coloring of the first keeper's house, as does the nearby fog horn building.

Behind and much farther above these buildings, the light tower surveys its domain from a clearing at the crest of the island's highest point. Built in 1903, the octagonal, 22-foot-tall tower is covered with horizontal wood shingles interrupted only by a doorway and a small, square window overlooking the precipice. The tower narrows slightly, then fans out to support the octagonal walkway and circular metal railing. The 12-sided lantern room still houses an operating beacon, while behind the lamp, metal panels revolve to provide a break in the beam of light, creating a flashing effect.

A small, modern pole light pokes up near the railing, and two antennae have also been added. They point to the crowning glory of the tower — a red beaver weathervane atop the ventilator ball, the animal always running against the wind.

Otter Island Light

O tter Island is a small, irregularly shaped strip of land poking up out of Lake Superior about 25 miles northwest of Michipicoten Island. The light here, established in 1903 on the northwest shore, is a 21-foot-tall, six-sided tower perched on a dark-gray rock outcropping. Its white surface is broken only by a few porthole windows, and the red walkway and lantern room provide a bright spot of color contrasting with the forest behind.

Closer to shore, a large, white two-story keeper's house sits near several other outbuildings, connected to each other and the tower by cement walkways edged by protective railings and slightly elevated to create safe, smooth paths over the island's rugged stone surface.

In front of the complex, the dark rock drops sharply nearly 25 feet to the shore. There, contrasting bands of light-tan and dark-gray rock disappear slowly beneath the water's surface, the lighter rock creating a halo of light beneath the greenish depths of Lake Superior.

Michipicoten Island Lighthouse

At 22 miles long and six miles wide, Michipicoten Island, 30 miles off the northeast shore of Lake Superior, is one of that lake's largest islands. The island's northeast shore angles gently down to large rock outcroppings that stretch out then dive beneath the turquoise waters. Between the rocks is a soft band of sand and gravel beach, and just behind it are the red-and-white buildings of the Michipicoten Island lightstation. Fronting the small outpost is the 71-foot-high white concrete tower, built in 1912, its round, red metal lantern room contrasting with the deep-green forest behind it. The hexagonal structure is supported by buttresses on each side, making its profile very similar to that of the Caribou Island light. Several surrounding buildings are connected by cement walkways to a small boat dock and helipad near shore.

Nature generously blessed the beautiful island with deposits of lead, copper, and silver. Agates, greenstone, and the occasional amethyst are also scattered throughout the interior and along the shore. "Michipicoten" originally meant Island of Hills, but early Native Americans also called it the "floating island," because of its peculiar quality of appearing to be far away one day and much closer the next.

Thirty miles northeast of the island, nestled along the rocky mainland shore of Michipicoten Harbor, is another beautiful lightstation, but its light tower is no longer standing.

Davieaux Island Light

The first light to guard Quebec Harbor, on the south side of large Michipicoten Island, was built in 1872 on the point protecting the harbor. A dwelling and two range lights were also constructed but on the harbor's opposite, north shore. Each evening Charles Davieaux, the first lightkeeper here, rowed across the harbor to service the larger light on the point, which required his spending the night at the light while his family tended the range lights close to home.

During Davieaux's stint here, a second rear range was built, also on the harbor's north shore, near the old range. Several years later the original light on the point was replaced by a light on a small, nearby island, which was renamed in the keeper's honor.

Today, that three-story light tower rises from green pines near the center of the narrow strip of land. Below the trees, black rock falls away to create a formidable barrier before slipping beneath the dark-green depths of Lake Superior. The hexagonal, white tower sports a row of square windows overlooking the water to the north and an entrance door topped by a pair of rectangular windows — all trimmed in red — on the south. Topping the structure are a red walkway and lantern room that surround an operational Fresnel lens.

Nearer the eastern end of the island, a large, white, two-story house is joined by a walkway to additional buildings farther east. The lower shoreline in this area is a flat expanse of reddish-gray stone that will tolerate no growth. A network of cracks race across the surface, creating giant paving stones. As the island narrows further, a helicopter pad and a few outbuildings are tucked into the last grove of forest.

Beyond this point, the rock stretches into a long finger, its tip gilded with a wide expanse of gold lichen and its rugged profile dotted with dark rocks projecting above the surface of the turquoise water. A solitary path snakes out to the tip of the island, where a small, white building stands isolated from the others, left to face the brunt of Lake Superior's fury without the comparative shelter of the pines farther inland.

" A network of cracks race across the surface, creating giant paving stones. "

Caribou Island Lighthouse

"Native Americans believed the island was guarded by a giant snake that kept a watchful eye over nuggets of gold."

The Caribou Island lighthouse complex completely fills a small island just southwest of the much larger main Caribou Island. From the air, the treacherous shoals that make travel so hazardous in this area are plainly seen, their long, brown fingers stretching out into the lake only feet beneath the turquoise waters of Lake Superior. Scraping over these shoals — which continue for miles — is believed by some to have been the cause of the sinking of the *Edmund Fitzgerald* in 1975.

The first light here was built in 1886 on the roof of the keeper's dwelling. Today's light tower, built in 1911, is a modern-looking steel-sheathed hexagonal structure with a row of small square windows running up one side. Distinctive flying buttresses that support the 82-foot-tall tower on four sides have open areas, giving the structure a distinctly futuristic look. A circular, red metal walkway at the top surrounds the lantern room, which is capped by a red dome and glazed 360 degrees with dozens of square panes that offer a breathtaking view of

Lake Superior and the nearby island.

A sturdy L-shaped cement dock angles out to provide Coast Guard personnel convenient access to the busy complex, which includes living quarters, several outbuildings, fuel tanks and solar panels. A small seawall separates the green lawns from the rugged gravel shoreline and protects the grass from the waves. And several trees that have flourished on a portion of the island offer some protection from the wind.

Protection has long been the theme of this island. Native Americans believed it was guarded by a giant snake that kept a watchful eye over nuggets of gold said to be scattered across the land. When European explorers heard the tale, they organized an expedition out to the remote island, determined to claim the gold. Fully believing the huge serpent was real, they drew their weapons as they approached the island. But they made it to shore and when they stepped out of their boat, they found no snake, no gold — only Caribou. They shot five of the animals during their three-day stay, and while returning to their boat, they were attacked by a flock of hawks. The beaten men left, disappointed that no part of the legend was true.

But perhaps there was a grain of truth. If the island had been infested with normal-size snakes (not uncommon on the Great Lakes), hawks would have been attracted to the easy pickings.

"From the air, the treacherous shoals are plainly seen, their long, brown fingers stretching out into the lake only feet beneath the turquoise waters of Lake Superior."

Corbeil Point Lighthouse

The once-busy Corbeil Point lighthouse is a square two-story structure that now shows disuse and neglect. The sloping roof covering the house is rusty, and the tower rises from the center of the roof to a missing lantern. Though this lighthouse stands just yards from the rocky shoreline of Lake Superior, you can't visit by land, as this area is part of an Indian Reservation, with no trespassing allowed. You can view the light from the water, however.

Nearby, behind a closed restaurant just north of Batchawana Bay, is the Coppermine Point light, which was removed from its original location.

Ile Parisienne Lighthouse

Ile Parisienne is a beautiful island framed by the turquoise blue waters of Lake Superior midway between Gros Cap, Ontario, and Whitefish Point, Michigan. Its pale brown shoreline changes from sand to gravel with every curve, and its interior is lush with the rich, deep greens of pines and scattered hardwoods.

Nearly 20 years before the island received a light, it was temporarily touched by a rather unusual developer. The man believed that the rugged, wild, isolated island was the perfect location for a beaver farm, especially since there was a small pond to provide habitat. In 1893 he brought several beaver to the island, then left for the winter. When he returned in the spring to a pond abandoned by the scattered family of beaver, he gave up on the idea.

In 1912 the lighthouse was built at the southwest corner of the island on a small peninsula barely wide enough to accommodate the tower and a few buildings. A 75-foot-long cement dock turns gracefully toward shore, continuing its line from that of a low cement wall curving around the peninsula's tip. Just in from the wall is the white, octagonal tower, with a small, red door at its base and a matching red walkway and lantern room 30 feet above. Square windows surround the lantern room, exposing it to the bright sunlight from any angle.

A red-and-white work building rests near the main dock, and a white, red-roofed house sitting closer to the peninsula's base has its own small dock. Another dwelling along the shoreline, nearly hidden by trees, provides additional living space. Solar panels are the power source for this isolated station, and a helipad makes for easier access.

> *"The man believed that the rugged, wild, isolated island was the perfect location for a beaver farm."*

Gros Cap Reefs Lighthouse

" The light's huge cement foundation is sharply angled at one end like the prow of a ship cutting through the waves. "

Since 1953 the red flashing beacon of the Gros Cap Reefs light has warned sailors of the dangerous reef stretching out from the tip of the Gros Cap Peninsula to the northeast. A wooden crib supports the light's huge cement foundation, sharply angled at one end like the prow of a ship cutting through the waves. A thick band of red runs along the base of the white foundation, and a square, white building is centered above. A slightly smaller room sits atop the first, and most windows in both levels have been sealed and painted red. Dominating the structure is a helicopter pad jutting out over the water near roof level and anchored to the foundation by a network of red, angled steel supports. A huge red-and-white radio antenna rises above the building.

You can see this light from either the Canadian or American side of the lake. In Canada the rocky shoreline of Gros Cap Peninsula provides a distant view of the light, while from Point Iroquois lightstation in Brimley, Michigan, you can see the reef light floating on the horizon.

Bellevue Park Old Range Light

" The doorway of the pilot house and windows of the cabin are just the right size for tiny bodies to wiggle through and pretend to pilot the powerful craft. "

Bellevue Park, east of downtown Sault Sainte Marie, includes Topsail Island, which is joined to the mainland across the St. Mary's River by a causeway. Near the island's southwest shore is the square, white pyramidal tower of the range light, its tapered wooden walls interrupted by only a few square windows trimmed in black and topped with small, angled overhangs. A square walkway with black railing surrounds the now-boarded-up lantern room.

On display near the light are other artifacts from the lakes. A huge wood and steel rudder lies at the edge of a clearing, with a backdrop of trees spreading out behind. A pretty, red tug has been stripped of its hull and placed near the riverbank, its black smokestack secured with long cables. A favorite of children, the doorway of the pilot house and windows of the cabin are just the right size for tiny bodies to wiggle through and pretend to pilot the powerful craft.

Other attractions and facilities at the park include a zoo, a picnic area, and beautiful flower gardens.

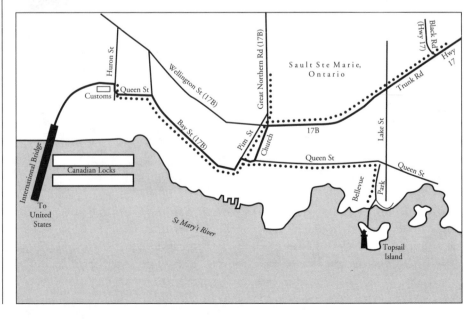

DIRECTIONS: If entering Canada from the U.S., turn right (south) as you leave the customs area and go ½ block to the traffic signal at Queen St. Turn left (east) and follow the Hwy. 17-B signs through the waterfront area (the road changes from Queen to Bay St. during this stretch). Approximately 1.7 miles (2.7 km.) after leaving customs, Hwy. 17-B curves left onto Pim St., at the Aircraft and Forest Fire Museums, and then in one block turns right (east) onto Queen St. About 1½ blocks farther, 17-B jogs left (north) onto Church St. Continue straight (east) on Queen and go about a mile (1.5 km.) to Bellevue Park, on the right just past the Ontario Forest Research Institute.

If entering Sault Ste. Marie from the north, follow Hwy. 17-B (Great Northern Rd.) to where it curves right (southwest) onto Pim St., near the downtown area. Follow Pim (one-way south), across Wellington St., about 0.2 mile (0.3 km.) to Queen St. Turn left (east) onto Queen and go about 1.1 miles (1.7 km.) to Bellevue park, on the right.

If entering Sault Ste. Marie from the east, take Hwy. 17 to where it turns north onto Black Rd. Continue straight (west), following Hwy. 17-B (first on Trunk Rd., then Wellington St.) approximately 1.7 miles (2.7 km.) to where 17-B turns north onto Church St. Continue straight (west) on Wellington one more block to Pim St. (one way south). Turn left (south) onto Pim and drive about 0.2 mile (0.3 km.) to Queen St. Turn left (east) onto Queen and go about 1.1 miles (1.7 km.) to Bellevue Park, on the right.

The old range light is at the south end of the park on Topsail Island, in the St. Mary's River.

Wilson Channel Range Lights

The Wilson Channel Ranges rest on a small strip of land cleared from the steep, wooded shore of Lake Huron's North Channel just across from St. Joseph Island. Established in 1905, the ranges are matching white, wooden towers nearly 30 feet tall, with a long, red stripe running from top to bottom. Each has a small, white walkway and red cap. The rear range stands about 200 yards from shore on rocky land that drops down past the front range to the water.

You can get a good view of these lights from a small roadside park just before crossing the Highway 548 bridge to St. Joseph Island.

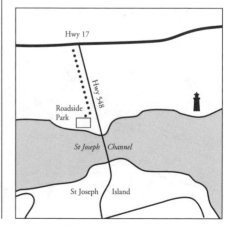

DIRECTIONS: Approximately 27.5 miles (44.3 km.) east of Sault Ste. Marie on Hwy. 17, turn right (south) onto Hwy. 548 to St. Joseph Island. At about 2.0 miles (3.2 km.), as you approach the bridge to the island, look for a roadside park on the right. Turn into the park and view the range lights, across the water to the east.

Shoal Island Lighthouse

"Towering pines stretch their twisted limbs over the stone surface toward a narrow, picturesque finger of stone."

Shoal Island is a small patch of land dotting the blue waters of Lake Huron less than a quarter mile off the northwest shore of much larger St. Joseph Island. Small rock outcroppings dominate Shoal Island's landscape, and towering pines stretch their twisted limbs over the stone surface toward a narrow, picturesque finger of stone on the north shore. There, where the trees end, the 34-foot-tall Shoal Island lighthouse stands guard, with only a few small bushes to keep it company. At the tip of the point, bare rock — tinged a pale gold where it touches the water's edge — slips quietly beneath the waves.

The white two-story house, built in 1885, is shingled in dark red, with the roof sloping down and off the rear of the structure and held up by corner pillars to create a covered porch. And what beautiful views must have greeted lightkeepers through the multipaned windows, which create a turn-of-the-century look. The beacon — a wide, square walkway surrounding the white lantern room and red cap —rises from the center of the house's roof.

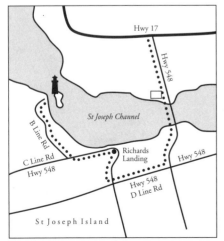

🗼 DIRECTIONS: From Hwy. 17 approximately 27.5 miles (44.3 km.) east of Sault Ste. Marie, turn right (south) onto Hwy. 548 and go about 3 miles (4.8 km.), crossing over the bridge, to a stop sign at D Line Rd. on St. Joseph Island. (Look for a store on the left at this intersection.) Turn right (west), continuing to follow Hwy. 548 (D Line Rd.) about 3.9 miles (6.3 km.)to C Line Rd. in the town of Richards Landing. (Hwy. 548 turns north at about **3** miles [5 km.].) Turn left (west) onto C Line (Hwy. 548) and go about one mile (1.6 km.) to B Line Rd. Turn right (north) onto B Line and go about 2.6 miles (4.2) km. to the road's end. (B Line is ashphalt for about 1.2 miles [1.9 km.], then gravel.) Look for the lighthouse, about ¼ mile (0.4 km.) out to the northeast.

West Sister Rock Light

West Sister Rock light is anchored to a small chunk of stone that narrowly accommodates the light and rises just far enough above the water to provide a sometimes-dry landing for a few gulls. The small, white tower is dwarfed by both the wide expanse of surrounding waters and the rolling hills of Ontario's mainland, less than a mile away. First lit in 1885, the six-sided structure narrows slightly as it rises more than 30 feet to a white walkway and red roof.

There is no good spot to view this light from shore.

McKay Island Lighthouse

Now privately owned, McKay Island is a small piece of land sitting in the blue waters of Lake Huron a mile from the town of Bruce Mines. Built in 1907, the lighthouse and several newer buildings dominate the eastern shoreline of the island. The house is a small, white wooden building with a square, red roof that slopes deeply downward to cover a small addition on the back of the structure. The walkway of the tower rests on the peak of the roof and surrounds the base of the unused lantern room.

A few yards closer to shore is a 30 foot-tall skeleton tower built to replace the older structure. A small, modern beacon rests at its top, and red day markers down the outside add the only other color.

Strawberry Island Lighthouse

The Strawberry Island lighthouse, established in 1881, sits at the northern edge of the 8-square-mile Georgian Bay island, close enough to the turquoise water to feel the splash from waves washing the gravelly shoreline. A fringe of grasses and small bushes line the shore, while behind the lighthouse a grove of towering hardwoods provides some shade.

The sides of the 40-foot-tall, white pyramidal tower are decorated with rows of red-trimmed windows, while the red walkway and lantern room dominate the top. Glass panes open up only the front half of the lantern room to view; the back is enclosed by siding.

Attached at the back of the tower is the white 1½-story keeper's house. The roof of a small addition angles down off the rear of the house, and a beautiful stone foundation supports the entire structure.

The lighthouse is currently leased to private individuals, and we urge consideration of their privacy.

> *"The lighthouse sits close enough to the turquoise water to feel the splash from waves washing the gravelly shoreline."*

Kagawong Light

The first light tower to guard the Kagawong harbor, at the tip of Mudge Bay on the north-central shore of Manitoulin Island, was built in 1880 at the end of a modest wood dock. A replacement light was built on the same spot in 1888 but lasted only four years before suddenly burning down. It took two years to replace the destroyed light with a square tower built on shore where it still stands today, separated from the bay by a road.

The 31-foot-tall, white wooden structure tapers as it rises to decorative supports that help hold the square walkway. Above is the square, red lantern room, and below, square windows peek out from beneath their own angled overhangs plus the larger overhang of the walkway.

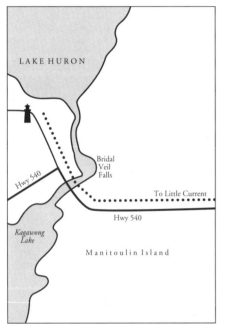

LAKE HURON

Hwy 540

Bridal
Veil
Falls

To Little Current

Hwy 540

Kagawong
Lake

Manitoulin Island

DIRECTIONS: To visit Manitoulin Island, go about 30 miles (48 km.) south of Espanola on Hwy. 6 to the swing bridge from Great LaCloche Island to Manitoulin Island. (The bridge opens each hour on the hour for approximately 15 minutes to allow boats to pass through.) Cross the bridge and go 0.5 mile (0.8 km.) farther on Hwy. 6 to the junction with Hwy. 540, in Little Current.

Turn right (west) onto Hwy. 540 and drive approximately 28 miles (45 km.) to where Hwy. 540 turns left, just past Bridal Veil Falls, on the right. Continue straight ahead 0.5 mile (0.8 km.) into Kagawong and look for the Kagawong light, on the left next to the road and across the street from a marina.

Janet Head Lighthouse

The Janet Head lighthouse (also known as the Gore Bay lighthouse) was built in 1879 on a point of land named by Lt. Bayfield, the surveyor of Lake Huron in the early 1800s, in honor of his daughter. Attached to the corner of the modest, white two-story house is the square, white 25-foot-tall tower. Pretty four- and six-paned windows illuminate the first and second levels, and a red-trimmed door near the base opens to a bright red, open porch and small stairway. The octagonal lantern room is guarded by a square, white fence and walkway, and inside, a modern beacon has replaced the Fresnel lens.

You can view the light — now a private residence that marks the entrance to the Janet Head Campground, near the town of Gore Bay — from the road nearby.

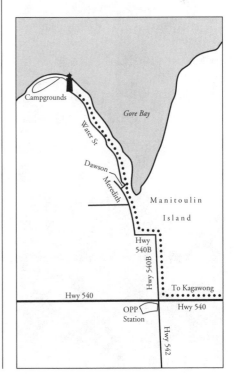

DIRECTIONS: On Manitoulin Island approximately 9 miles (14.5 km.) west of Kagawong (see DIRECTIONS, p. 112) on Hwy. 540, turn right (north) onto Hwy. 540-B (look for an O.P.P. Station on the southwest corner of this intersection) and go about 1.5 miles (2.4 km.) to Meredith St. in Gore Bay. Continue straight ahead (north) on Meredith 0.2 mile (0.3 km.), through the downtown area, to Dawson St. Turn right (east) onto Dawson and go one block to Water St. Turn left (north) onto Water and go to its end, at the campgrounds, about 1.5 miles (2.4 km.) past the point where the road turns to gravel. Janet Head lighthouse is on the left, just before the campgounds.

Mississagi Straits Lighthouse Museum

"The inside of the lighthouse has been converted into a fascinating museum."

The Mississagi Straits lighthouse, built in 1873, sits on a section of flat, white rock with just the slightest hint of lawn poking out in tufts from the pock-marked stone. From a lakeside corner of the two-story frame house, the square, wood tower rises just eight feet above the roofline before supporting a square walkway that provides a wide border around the narrow, octagonal lantern room.

Attached to the back of the house is a one-story addition with its own tall chimney protruding from a dark red roof matching that of the main building. An even-smaller room off the end of the addition completes the long house. Tall cedars shade one side of the building, and sweeping down to the shore are thick bushes mixed with a few tall birch and cedar silhouetted against the sky.

The inside of the lighthouse has been converted into a fascinating museum, with replica furnishings in each room giving an authentic 19th-century feel to the lightstation. In the living room, for instance, comfortable chairs snuggle close to a potbellied stove. And the simple dining table and chairs speak of the plain but nourishing fare that must have been served here.

You can also climb the light tower, which shows its age in the chipped and cracked paint along the inside of the red metal lantern room. A partial piece of the fragile lens that once warned of the straits and the area's magnetic reefs is now illuminated by a simple light bulb tilted at an angle.

And on display inside a small boathouse sitting behind the lighthouse at the

edge of the bluff are oak beams from a ship found on the shoreline nearby and believed to be the remains of the Great Lakes' first shipwreck, LaSalle's *Griffon*.

The lighthouse complex, named Heritage Park and Campground, is currently leased to the Meldrum Bay Historical Society, which opens and runs the facility — including the museum plus a restaurant in the lightstation's old foghorn building — during the summer months.

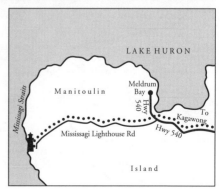

DIRECTIONS: On the western end of Manitoulin Island approximately one mile before entering Meldrum Bay on Hwy. 540, turn left (west) onto Mississagi Lighthouse Rd. This road is well-marked, and from Hwy. 540 it is approximately 6.5 miles (10.5 km.) (the last 3.5 miles are good gravel road) to the lighthouse museum.

Manitowaning Light

"*The bay is visible as a twisting ribbon of blue far below.*"

The Manitowaning light, established in 1885 on a bluff high above the west side Manitowaning Bay, has the familiar shape and construction of many of Canada's lights: a white, wooden, pyramidal tower topped with a square walkway and red, octagonal lantern room. A set of stairs runs up a few feet to meet the door set into the base of the 35-foot-tall tower.

A modern beacon within the lantern room still guides boaters into the safety of the bay, visible as a twisting ribbon of blue far below.

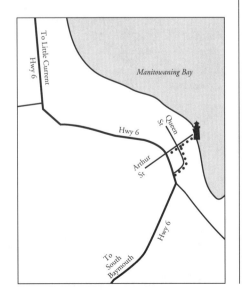

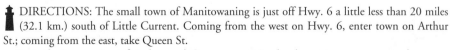 DIRECTIONS: The small town of Manitowaning is just off Hwy. 6 a little less than 20 miles (32.1 km.) south of Little Current. Coming from the west on Hwy. 6, enter town on Arthur St.; coming from the east, take Queen St.

From the intersection of Arthur and Queen streets in the downtown area, go northwest on Arthur one block and look for the harbor light on the right.

South Baymouth Range Lights

Built in 1898, the South Baymouth range lights rest along a shore reinforced with a low stone wall along the water's edge plus a second, taller wall a few yards back. The lights are nearly identical: white, wood towers angling upward to support square, wooden walkways and lanterns with red caps. Both are marked with a long, red stripe running nearly the height of their front walls to provide day markers for ships approaching the area. The 17-foot tall front range stands close to the water, and the 26-foot-tall rear range is about 250 yards inland, nearly hidden by tall trees.

Nearby in South Baymouth, you can catch the car ferry *Chi-Cheemaun* for an enjoyable two-hour cruise to Tobermory, on the tip of the Bruce Peninsula. The trip includes some of the most beautiful scenery on the Great Lakes, including views of the Cove Island lighthouse. The ferry is equipped with a restaurant, gift shop, and plenty of deck chairs. For a schedule and fares, call the Tobermory Terminal at (519) 596-2510 or the South Baymouth Terminal at (705) 859-3161.

> " *The lights rest along a shore reinforced with a low stone wall along the water's edge plus a second, taller wall a few yards back.* "

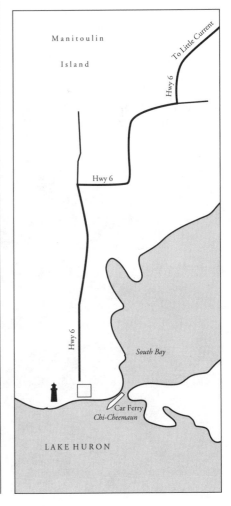

DIRECTIONS: From Little Current on Manitoulin Island, go approximately 39 miles (63 km.) south on Hwy. 6 to its end at the ferry dock in South Baymouth. The front range light is near the water's edge, just west of the public marina. The rear range light is about 250 yards behind the front range and, although on private property, can be seen from the roadway.

Great Duck Island Lighthouse

" A wide band of dark gray gravel forms the beach and helps muffle the crashing Lake Huron waves. "

The interior of Great Duck Island, 12 miles south of Manitoulin Island, is a mixture of heavy pines and cedars striped with an occasional hardwood. A wide band of dark gray gravel forms the beach and helps muffle the crashing Lake Huron waves.

The lighthouse complex sprawls across a large section of cleared land on the 7-square-mile island's southwest side. Closest to shore is a modern connection to the outside world — a helipad. Farther inland, a cluster of abandoned foundations, fuel tanks, and a power house marks the front of the station. Backing up against the thick wall of forest at the rear is the two-story keeper's house, while just 50 feet away, a thick stone foundation and steps are the only remains of a once-busy former dwelling. Fifty feet farther south is a modern, white one-story building, and next to it a foundation whose stone marks the remains of yet another former building.

Rising far above all those structures and small trees is the light tower, an 85-foot-tall white concrete octagon with a row of rectangular windows running up two sides to illuminate the interior stairway. A red, octagonal metal walkway surrounds the completely glazed lantern room, with each of its 10 panes affording a magnificent view of the island or the surrounding blue waters of Lake Huron.

Killarney Northwest Light

The first light on Partridge Island, in Lake Huron just west of the village of Killarney, was established in 1866 along with the Killarney East lighthouse on shore. The small lighthouse that stands on the island today is identical to many of Canada's smaller lights. It is a white, wooden pyramid topped with a square, red metal walkway surrounding an octagonal lantern room with red cap and ventilator ball.

But the distinctive surroundings of this light set it apart. Inland, pines cover the land with a mass of twisted limbs, with small shrubs squeezing into any unoccupied space. At the shoreline, the flora vanishes, leaving the beautiful gold and gray rock to challenge the power of Lake Huron on its own. Out from shore, small wisps of the same smooth rock peek up shyly above the surface, all but invisible during periods of high water — beautiful, but another hazard in this treacherous bay.

You can visit this light aboard a water taxi, which will pick you up from any Killarney area dock. For more information call Georgian Bay Charters, run by Captain Darcy Noble, at (705) 287-2709.

" The distinctive surroundings of this light set it apart. "

119

Killarney East Lighthouse

"The rocks of Killarney seem almost liquid."

The Killarney East lighthouse, established in 1866, rests on a beautiful promontory of golden brown rock 30 feet above the blue waters of Georgian Bay. The stone slopes gently down to the shoreline, its smooth, water-worn face marred by cracks and fissures. These rocks of Killarney seem almost liquid, with gentle curves that slip quietly beneath the waves on one side, while on the other they look like huge red and black building blocks tumbling haphazardly into the water.

Rising up 25 feet from the rock is the picturesque lighthouse, a square, white, wooden tower topped by a square, red metal walkway surrounding the partially glazed lantern room. A complex radio tower poking up from the walkway an additional five feet above the roof adds a modern footnote to the otherwise nostalgic location. Closer to shore, two small buildings hide beneath the sheltering arms of a pine and are protected from the water by a concrete wall. Out from shore, small rock outcroppings raise their smooth surface barely a foot above the water, creating a great hazard for boats venturing into the area.

DIRECTIONS: From Hwy. 69 about midway between Sudbury and French River, turn west onto Hwy. 637 and go approximately 40 miles (67 km.) to Killarney. As you enter the village, initially follow the signs to the airport by turning left (east) on Ontario St. and driving about 0.6 mile (1 km.) to where it turns left, at the junction with a gravel road, to the airport.

The lighthouse is about ½ mile (0.8 km.) straight ahead (east) on the gravel two-track. You can either walk in or drive in a little more than halfway, then walk. If you drive, at about 0.3 mile (0.5 km.) you will reach a parking area just before where the road is gated. (The two-track road is in very good condition to this point but is hardly wide enough to pass another car in most spots. Therefore, we do not recommend driving in in recreational vehicles.) From the gate it is about a ¼-mile (0.4-km.) walk down the two-track to the lighthouse.

You can also view this light from aboard the Killarney water taxi. See the Killarney Northwest lighthouse text, page 119, for details.

French River
Inner Range Lights

The French River Front Range light — a circular, white 15-foot-tall tower marked with an orange vertical stripe — stands on narrow Lefroy Island in the mouth of the river.

On the mainland about ¾ mile upriver is the French River Rear Range light, a small, white tower just 15 feet tall, with a red stripe running down its front and topped with a small red cap. This unassuming light is surrounded by some of the Great Lakes most beautiful country. Behind it, a thick stand of young trees blends into grasses and bushes that stretch down to the rocky shore-line. A thin strip of exposed gray and white stone runs along the shore, its smooth face dotted with the golden lichen predominant in the area. Farther

FRENCH RIVER REAR RANGE

"The lumber company began stacking their products in front of the light."

along the shore, the land rises to great hills topped with towering pines, their branches fanned out against the deep blue sky. But no color anywhere can match the deep velvet-blue of the French River, which cuts a wide swath through the multicolored rock and fragrant, deep green forests of Ontario wilderness before emptying into Georgian Bay.

Looking at the beautiful blanket of pines now surrounding the rear range, it's hard to imagine that a century ago, the area was devoid of trees. Instead, a bustling town stretched along the shore, and in 1875 a pair of range lights began guiding vessels into the busy river. One of the first lightkeepers here, Edward Borron Jr., performed his duties conscientiously including, in 1882, warning his superiors of a potential problem. After spotting lumber company surveyors on the riverbanks surrounding the rear range light, Borron recommended procuring a few acres as a "buffer zone" so that, if his speculation were correct, future piles of lumber would not obscure the light.

His suggestion, however, was ignored and within a year, when the lumber company began stacking their products for easy shipment at the rivermouth in front of the light, complaints flooded in to the Department of Marine and Fisheries. The lumber company truthfully replied that their piles did not block the beacon. Government officials were about to breathe heavy sighs of relief when Borron again wrote and explained that ships' pilots must be able to see not only the beam from the lamp, but also the entire tower, which was used as a day marker.

Finally, seven years and numerous complaints later, the Department of Marine, apparently deciding the problem wasn't going away, investigated. Nine years after Borron had made his initial recommendation, an official finally validated it by concluding that "a great deal of this trouble has arisen from the fact that we did not have a survey made of the lighthouse reserve required." The government must have taken action, however, for the complaints soon stopped.

But the lights turned out to be troublesome in other ways, and in 1900 further changes were made. The rear range's beam, for instance, was so weak that it was necessary to change from a 6.5-inch to 15-inch reflector. Also, the front range on Lefroy Island was difficult to distinguish from the rear range, so its beacon was changed from white to red.

Lightkeepers here also had to row the short distance to Lefroy Island to light and service the front range lamp each night. Most believed their biggest potential danger to be the cold, dark waters, should their boat capsize. But one day in the early years of this century, when lightkeeper Bob Young was rowing out to the island, a hunter's stray bullet struck him, injuring his hand, arm and side. Having no other options, he rowed back to shore and got help. After recovering at the Parry Sound Hospital, Young returned to work only to have thieves break into his house and burglarize it while he was servicing the front range light.

The range lights are still operational, but only pleasure boats move up the river and the rivermouth shoreline is again wilderness hiding the few remains of the once-thriving town there.

FRENCH RIVER FRONT RANGE

Bustard Rocks Range and Northeast Range Lights

Three miles out from the French River entrance, a collection of smooth, gray stones rises no more than 10 feet above the lake to form the small land mass known as Bustard Rocks. Gentle dips and swells run across its face, creating footholds for patches of lush, green grass, while closer to the waterline, gold lichen clings to the rock's smooth surface.

The presence of three range lights on such a tiny clump of rock makes this a most unusual area in the Great Lakes. Established in 1875, the lights, along with the French River Inner Range lights, were deemed necessary to help mariners with the difficult approach to the French River. The Bustard Rocks Northeast Rear Range light is a square 30-foot-tall tower that narrows as it rises to support a walkway and red lantern room. The Bustard Rocks Range and Northeast Range Front lights are identical 20-foot-tall pyramidal towers topped with a small, red, square cap. A small home was also built on the island for the keeper's use but is no longer standing.

The first keeper here was Edward Borron, who was succeeded 10 years later by his son, Edward, Jr. Like most other lightkeepers, Edward Jr. was resourceful. In 1900 for instance, when ship captains complained that the range lights became temporarily obscured during their approaches, Borron solved the problem by shortening the window sash and putting in a larger pane of glass.

When Edward Borron, Jr. died suddenly in 1902, the government allowed Mrs. Borron and their six children to care for the lights. Two sons were old enough to row out to the island lights each night, leaving behind an anxious mother each time, and ultimately, the Borron family kept the lights another 17 years.

A later keeper, Thomas William Flynn, is still remembered for his attempts to beautify the near-bare Bustard Rocks. He and his family hauled over loads of dirt, mixed it with the manure of chickens raised on the island, and created some of the area's most beautiful vegetable gardens and flowers beds.

"The presence of three range lights on such a tiny clump of rock makes this a most unusual area in the Great Lakes."

92

Byng Inlet Range Lights

The Byng Inlet Front Range light, built in 1890 along with the rear range light, is a small 34-foot-tall white, pyramidal tower surrounded at its base by dense, low-growing shrubs. A lone narrow window affords a limited view of the surroundings, and above it a small, white walkway supports an unusual lantern room. The square room is completely enclosed, with a tiny, modern beacon poking out of the front. A wide, red, vertical stripe runs up the front of the wood tower from the boarded-up entrance door to the top of the lantern room.

The white metal skeleton of the Rear Range light angles up to support a large, red enclosed room topped with a walkway surrounding a square, red lantern room whose cap is 60 feet above the rock below.

The shoreline in front of both range lights is a strip of smooth, rounded rock, with just enough hollows and cracks to allow a patchy blanket of wild grasses to retain their hold while the deep blue waters of the inlet wash softly over them.

FRONT RANGE

REAR RANGE

Gereaux Island Lighthouse

Gereaux is a typical Georgian Bay island — its smooth, rounded stone surface rising not over 10 feet above the waves, leaving just enough space in a few areas for a light carpet of wild grasses.

Established in 1870 close to the north shore of the island, the Gereaux Island lighthouse marks the south side of the entrance to Byng Inlet. The structure is a replica of the Strawberry Island light — a square, wooden tower angling upward 40 feet to support a red metal walkway and lantern room. The attached two-story keeper's house and a one-story addition at the rear of that dwelling are both roofed with red shingles. All of the many rectangular windows of the house and tower are trimmed in red, and all are now sealed.

Several yards in front of the light is a 100-foot-high red-and-white radio tower, anchored and stabilized with several long guy wires. Not far inland, a white two-story Candian Coast Guard search-and-rescue station is bordered by a cluster of pines.

Pointe au Baril Range Lighthouse

" This body of land got its name from its first light. To guide boats into the dangerous channel here, early residents set a lantern atop a barrel. "

The Pointe Au Baril Front Range lighthouse sits at the edge of a Georgian Bay peninsula whose rocky profile is broken only here and there by young pines trying to gain a foothold on the rugged surface. Many lighthouses take the names of the bodies of land on which they stand, but this body of land got its name from its first light. To guide boats into the dangerous channel here, early residents set a lantern atop a barrel. Years later, they made improvements to the crude beacon — the top and bottom of the barrel were removed, it was turned on its side, and the lantern was placed inside. Thus, sailors could only see the light when they looked at the barrel straight on, making this a unique range light.

In 1889 "real" range lights were built here, and both are still standing. The front range lighthouse is built on a beautiful stone foundation that, because the structure is set into a hill, is most apparent beneath the tower, which is closest to the water's edge. The keeper's dwelling is a modest 1½-story white house with a bright red roof and matching trim. A short, enclosed walkway connects the house to the square, white 30-foot-high tower, which narrows as it rises. Bright red overhangs cap the narrow windows of the walkway and the tower plus the doorway at its base. The red is repeated on the wide platform and railing surrounding the six-sided lantern room and its cap.

The rear range light is a 22-foot-tall steel tower on nearby Macklin Island.

Both ranges were constructed by Charles Mickler who, like most builders before and since, probably welcomed the government contract. But when Mickler completed the Pointe Au Baril lights plus the Narrow Island light, government officials claimed he had not satisfied conditions of the contract and refused to pay. Mickler sued the Dominion Government and won. In 1893, four years after he had finished the Pointe Au Baril construction, he finally received payment for both.

But amazingly, neither he nor the government learned from the experience. In 1894 Mickler signed contracts to build the Jones Island and Snug Harbor lights. Upon completion of those projects, the building inspector condemned the work. Again the government refused to pay, again Mickler sued, and again he won.

Government involvement in finances proved to be a problem of a different sort for Samuel Edward Oldfield, the first lightkeeper at Pointe Au Baril. Oldfield tried to make ends meet by being both lightkeeper and master of a fishing boat. However, the difficulties and perhaps temptations of what is now called "double dipping" soon became apparent. During his first summer, while Oldfield was supposedly in Parry Sound buying building materials, a government boat dropped off supplies. When Oldfield reported that a tin of white lead had mysteriously disappeared from the dock before he "returned," the Department of Marine grew suspicious.

Not long after, in 1894, officials confirmed their suspicions and slapped Oldfield's hand as he again apparently reached for their cookie jar. Oldfield had submitted a bill for new sails for the station's boat. Because sails were expected to last

six to eight years, the government refused to pay, writing, "The Chief Engineer reports that on his last visit to your station, you were away in the sail boat on private business. Probably the short life of the sails may be due to many other trips of a like character."

Red Rock Light

As its name suggests, this light rests on a flat section of red sandstone smoothed by centuries of waves rolling over its surface. The exposed section of rock is small, only about three times the diameter of the round tower anchored securely to it. The base of the tower is painted bright red, the rest white. The top of the 42-foot-tall structure is a flat, red-and-white helicopter pad resting on four short skeleton legs that leave enough space for a small, red lantern room to be tucked in underneath.

Originally established in 1870, the tower marks the entrance to the main channel to Parry Sound.

Jones Island Range Lighthouse

Over the centuries, a few deep pockets in the dark brown stone of Jones Island have trapped enough soil to support strings of bushes and small pines. But near the 50-foot-tall lighthouse, the rock is almost completely bare, making the small, two-story structure appear even more isolated than it is. The red roof of the plain, white lighthouse is the only spot of bright color across the landscape, standing out against the deep green of the pines and turquoise waters of Georgian Bay. The light tower rises from the roof of the house, its square walkway supporting a beacon that, along with a companion light on nearby Gordon Rocks, still helps ships set a range for the channel leading to Parry Sound.

The range lights on Jones Island and Gordon Rocks were established in 1894.

" The red roof of the plain white lighthouse is the only spot of bright color across the landscape. "

Snug Harbour Range Lighthouse

"The gables are miniature roofs that angle steeply and briefly down."

Since 1894 the south end of Snug Island has been home to Snug Harbour's rear range lighthouse. Its companion light is farther offshore on Walton Island.

The Snug Harbour Rear Range lighthouse is a large, white structure with a distinctive red roofline. The gables of the two-story dwelling — instead of open and peaked — are miniature roofs that angle steeply and briefly down. The square, white tower rises from the center of the house's roof, narrowing to a square, red walkway that surrounds a much smaller, square, red lantern room. Inside, a warning beacon still shines across the blue waters of Georgian Bay.

Marking the very edge of the shoreline in front of the lighthouse are the concentric red-and-white circles of a helipad, and towering over the complex nearby is a huge radio antenna.

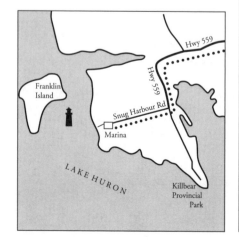

DIRECTIONS: From Hwy. 69 approximately 8 miles (12.9 km.) north of Parry Sound, turn west onto Hwy. 559 and go about 9.5 miles (15.2 km.) — jogging left (south) at 6.3 miles — to Snug Harbor Rd. Turn right (west) onto Snug Harbor Rd. and drive about 3.1 miles (5 km.) to its end at the Snug Harbor Marina. (About 0.1 mile [0.2 km.] before the end of the road, you will approach a Y junction. Continue straight ahead on the left fork, toward the boat dock and marina in view. Do not go up the hill on the right fork.) You can view the lighthouse, out in the harbor to the right, from the end of the boat dock.

Western Islands Lighthouse

The Western Islands are a small cluster of pale gray rocks protruding not over a dozen feet above the deep green waters 31 miles north of Collingwood, which marks the southern tip of Georgian Bay. The islands' rough stone surfaces are too harsh to allow even the smallest green plant a foothold; only a heavy dusting of deep gold lichen clings to the cracks.

The islands have been guarded since 1895 by the small, white, octagonal 45-foot-tall light tower poking up from Double Top Island. A wide band of bright red runs around the tower's base, matching the color of the walkway and lantern room. A narrow cement walkway crosses over the island's uneven stone to join the tower to a helicopter pad and another small building. And a tiny cement bridge joins this island with another just a few feet away.

" Only a heavy dusting of deep gold lichen clings to the cracks. "

131

Hope Island Lighthouse

Hope Island lies about a mile off the north shore of much larger Christian Island. The northeastern tip of Hope Island is devoted to a sprawling Coast Guard station that includes a helipad, a long dock, and several scattered buildings. The lighthouse, established in 1884, stands in the center of the complex and is very similar to that on Strawberry Island except for one glaring difference — the absence of the lantern room. The white pyramidal tower rises 40 feet to a flat platform devoid of the beacon that once proudly shone over the beautiful turquoise waters of Georgian Bay. The dwelling is attached to the tower, and two small one-story additions lean on opposite ends of the structure. All roofs are shingled in red, and a row of dark windows runs up the side of the tower. Nearby, a small skeleton tower supports a modern beacon, and a tall red-and-white radio tower rises behind the original lighthouse.

A network of sidewalks connects the lighthouse with the other buildings, including a large red-and-white structure with a platform supporting fuel tanks.

The shoreline is strewn with large boulders, making for a very rough waterline that necessitates the long, large dock behind the complex. A fringe of trees west of the lighthouse provides a band of dark green to contrast with the much lighter color of the grasses surrounding the buildings.

Brebeuf Range Lighthouse & Beausoleil Rear Range Light

Brebeuf Island is a small section of smooth stone thrust up from the depths of Lake Huron seven miles north of Midland, Ontario. Its surface is marred by long cracks and fissures, and small dips have collected enough earth to support a cluster of trees plus occasional small clumps of bushes. The only other vegetation is a pale gold line of lichen near the water's edge.

The design of the 35-foot-tall Front Range light is typical: a square tower angling upward to support a wide walkway and lantern room, each painted bright red. A small house is attached to the base of the tower, with a small room added on to the rear of the dwelling. The bright red of the lantern room is echoed in the red tiled roof of the house, creating a bright splash of color against the surrounding pale rocks. The only beach is a small gravel area behind the house where a small dock stretches out to accommodate Coast Guard personnel.

Not more than a quarter mile east, on the west shore of Beausoleil Island, the 88-foot-tall Rear Range rises above the dense foliage covering that island. The white skeleton tower rises to a square, white walkway surrounding the red lantern room. In front of the light, two small projections of rock spill out into the lake, creating a beautiful landmark of pale brown stone covered in a dusting of soft, green grass. And a small section of sand beach provides access to light-keepers venturing over from Brebeuf Island.

BREBEUF RANGE LIGHTHOUSE

BEAUSOLEIL REAR RANGE LIGHT

The Imperial Towers

" All six locations are beautiful destinations, and two — Cove Island and Point Clark — are spectacular. "

The sparkling waters around the Bruce Peninsula and into southern Georgian Bay are guarded by six beautiful lighthouses that share architectural style and builder. Collectively they are known as the Imperial Towers.

The reason for the name "Imperial" is lost to historians. Perhaps the structures were so titled in formal documents because the government paid for them with Imperial Treasury funds. Or someone may simply have first used the word as an appropriate description of the distinguished structures' strength and royal profile.

In the early 1850s, the government awarded the contract to build these lighthouses to John Brown, an unassuming yet successful and well-known builder from Thorold, Ontario. Originally from Scotland, Brown had spent six years as a stone mason in upstate New York before coming to Ontario, in 1838. There he opened a limestone quarry and then slowly began to build a business empire. During the mid-1840s, for instance, his company built portions of the second Welland Canal and also the Mohawk Island lighthouse in Lake Erie.

Constructing the new group of lighthouses, however, was the most challenging project Brown had faced. During the five years of construction, he dealt with isolated locations, sudden storms, and a labor force made recalcitrant by the hardships of working on the islands. When he finished in 1859, Brown was far over budget, leaving him with no profit, only the satisfaction that he had served his government and the sailors of upper Canada to the best of his abilities.

All six Imperial Towers still stand — on Chantry Island, Griffith Island, Nottawasaga Island, Christian Island, Point Clark, and Cove Island. Years of disinterest plus rough weather have, unfortunately, taken a toll on some of the keeper's dwellings and other buildings, in some cases destroying them. Still, all six locations are beautiful destinations for lighthouse enthusiasts, and two — Cove Island and Point Clark — are spectacular.

Christian Island Lighthouse

T he Christian Island lighthouse, one of the Imperial Towers, was first lit in 1859. The rugged stone walls of the light tower still appear powerful after all these years, but the ravages of time, and inattention have irrevocably changed the once-busy lightstation. The round tower still sports a fresh coat of whitewash, and a few narrow windows are set into its thick walls. At the top, the tower flares out slightly to support a walkway, but unfortunately the original railing and lantern room have been removed. A short, red metal railing runs along the top of the tower, and a small modern beacon is anchored to a rough platform, all that remains of the lantern room's support.

Nearby, the keeper's dwelling rises out of a mass of green bushes. The rough, gray stone walls have lost their windows and roof and are in danger of collapsing. The ruins' only protection is a dapple of shade from a hardwood planted by the keepers of long ago. A gravelly shoreline separates both the tower and house from the deep blue waters of Lake Huron several yards away.

Though life at almost all lighthouses was usually busy, the personality and attitude of the keeper largely determined how successfully each station would be cared for. The lightkeeper here in 1888 evidently was not particularly diligent in matters of maintenance. When he wrote an inspector asking for a new fence, the request was granted, but with comments in an official report that "I cannot help

"If a man cannot put up a board fence without assistance, he is not worth much."

DIRECTIONS: To get to the Christian Island ferry dock, follow Hwy. 93 north into the downtown area of Penetanguishene. As Hwy. 93 starts downhill toward the water you will come to a traffic signal at Robert St. Turn left (west) onto Robert and go about 1.2 miles (1.9 km.) to LaFontaine Rd. From this junction, follow Hwy. 26 to the ferry dock as follows. Turn right (north) onto LaFontaine Rd. and drive about 2.6 miles (4.2 km.) to a three-way stop. Turn left (west), continuing to follow LaFontaine, and go about 2 miles (3.2 km.) to a blinker light at the junction of LaFontaine Rd. and Hwy. 6. Continue straight, staying on LaFontaine and go approximately 2 miles (3.2 km.) (passing through the village of LaFontaine) to Cedar Point Rd. Turn right (north) onto Cedar Point Rd. and go about 1.7 miles (2.7 km.) to Tiny Con 18 Rd. Turn left (west) onto Tiny Con 18 Rd. and drive approximately 0.8 mile (1.3 km.) to where Hwy. 26 turns north. (The route is marked with a sign to the ferry.) Turn right (north) and go about 2.9 miles (4.7 km.) to the entrance road to the ferry. Turn left (west) and follow the signs about 0.4 mile (0.6 km.) down a hill to the ferry dock.

135

feeling to a certain extent the repairs are required through carelessness and shiftlessness on the part of the keeper."

Two years later, the keeper finally had a workman erect the fence and then billed the government for the man's $2.50 wages. But the keeper's superiors refused, writing in an internal memo, "If a man cannot put up a board fence without assistance, he is not worth much." Perhaps contributing to their disdain was the fact that in the same letter in which the keeper had tried to bill the government for the fence, he also submitted an invoice for a buoy he had placed, even after he had charged local ship captains for the cost.

Nottawasaga Island Lighthouse

The tall, white tower of the Nottawasaga Island lighthouse rises 95 feet into the blue sky, dwarfing the row of trees and shrubs that line the shore. The low-lying island, now a bird sanctuary, attracts hundreds of gulls, herons, mallards and cormorants. The cormorants exact a heavy toll, apparent in dozens of branches devoid of greenery.

The tall tower, however, is unmarked and shows no sign of deterioration. Narrow, red-trimmed windows look out across Georgian Bay and Collingwood Harbor, and at the top a red railing surrounds the beautiful lantern room. Dozens of square panes make up the lantern room from top to bottom, creating an open view, and a domed red metal cap and ventilator ball protect it from the elements.

One of the six Imperial Towers, the Nottawasaga lighthouse began operating in 1858 to warn those entering Collingwood Harbor of the area's dangerous reefs and ledges. In 1959 the tower was automated, and keepers were no longer required to live on the island.

The first keeper — stationed here in 1855 while the tower was being built — would hang a lighted lantern each night from the unfinished structure. The first permanent keeper was Captain George Collins, who came to the island in 1859. The captain was a first-rate lightkeeper, evidenced in an astounding record of more than 50 lives saved during his 31 years at the station. His courage was echoed in his son, an assistant lightkeeper who helped during rescues. In just one instance in 1872 when the steamer *Mary Ward* ran aground on a reef two miles from the light, Collins and his son rescued 24 people who otherwise would have perished in the frigid waters. Tragically, the younger Collins later drowned while fishing the same reef.

" In just one instance, Collins and his son rescued 24 people who otherwise would have perished. "

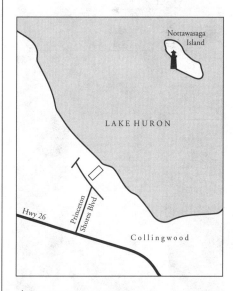

DIRECTIONS: From Hwy. 26 at the southern edge of Collingwood, turn north (toward the lake) onto Princeton Shores Blvd. and go about 0.2 mile (0.3 km.) to a stop sign. Turn left and, just around the corner look for a tennis court on the right. You can view the Nottawasaga Island lighthouse, about a mile out from shore, from the tennis court property near the water.

Griffith Island Lighthouse

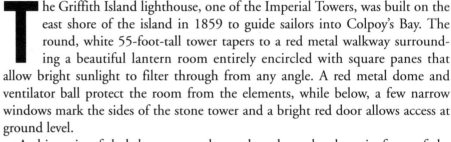

"The beautiful lake stretches along the shore like a bolt of aquamarine silk."

The Griffith Island lighthouse, one of the Imperial Towers, was built on the east shore of the island in 1859 to guide sailors into Colpoy's Bay. The round, white 55-foot-tall tower tapers to a red metal walkway surrounding a beautiful lantern room entirely encircled with square panes that allow bright sunlight to filter through from any angle. A red metal dome and ventilator ball protect the room from the elements, while below, a few narrow windows mark the sides of the stone tower and a bright red door allows access at ground level.

A thin strip of dark brown gravel stretches along the shore in front of the lighthouse, while farther east a section of low land has collected several large, shallow pools only yards from the lake. Though the deep emerald green of the surrounding thick forest stops just short of the lighthouse at remnants of cleared land, the trees are quickly reclaiming that area. In front of the lighthouse a row of bushes bend toward the beautiful lake, which stretches along the shore like a bolt of aquamarine silk.

Just a few yards from the tower is the abandoned keeper's house, the bright paint long gone from its dull gray stone walls. The roof is still intact, although it appears probably not for long, and a thick ring of bushes have grown around the house, nearly hiding it from view at water level. During the house's active years, lightkeepers and their families lived here eight months of the year, and at least one augmented his income by also commercially fishing.

For many years the lighthouse keepers had company — picnickers who journeyed over in boats from the mainland. And at night, animals — especially deer — would leave their daytime hiding places to search out the bright beacon, standing in the well lit yard.

Unfortunately, not all experiences were so pastoral. The last keeper here was a Mr. Bennet, who lived on the island with his mother. Bennet — who had only one leg as the result of a World War I injury — left one day to get supplies on the mainland but never returned. All that was recovered was his small boat.

Meaford Light Museum

Poking up from the roof of the Meaford Museum building is one of the most unusual light setups we have seen. From the early 1900s, a breakwater light helped guide boats into Meaford's harbor. When the government decided to add a rear range, they frugally placed it on top of a pump house that had been in use since 1895. A simple metal frame with a light atop was secured to one end of the pump house's roof peak.

Today, still bolted to the roof, a ladder with railings leads from the eaves up to the light, and a smaller metal ladder reaches down the side of the building to the ground. That this unique light is still standing speaks of the pride the residents of the small town of Meaford, Ontario, have for their history. Inside the building, which has been home to the museum since 1961, are pioneer displays from the 1800s.

" Poking up from the roof of the Meaford Museum building is one of the most unusual light setups we have seen."

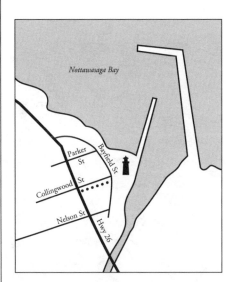

DIRECTIONS: From Hwy. 26 (Sykes St.) in Meaford, turn east toward Lake Huron onto Collingwood St. and go about 0.2 mile (0.3 km.) to Bayfield St. The museum is across Bayfield and to the left.

Cape Croker Lighthouse

"A Fresnel lens shows clearly through the windows."

The first lighthouse was built at this north entrance to Colpoy's Bay in 1898, and in 1902 the Cape Croker light that still stands today was built on a sharp rise near the Georgian Bay shoreline. Dominating the smooth, white eight-sided tower is the beautiful, huge lantern room enclosed by dozens of square glass panes. A Fresnel lens shows clearly through the windows, its green beam stretching over the water below. Supporting the lantern room is a red steel-sided room surrounded by a red railing. That room in turn stands on an octagonal platform — also with a red railing — that overhangs the tower walls. Just below that walkway is a rectangular window with thick, red trim, and added to the base of the tower is a tiny access room, its sloping roof barely topping the red entry door. The 53-foot-high structure is capped by a red dome topped with a weathervane.

This still-active lightstation includes a small, white one-story keeper's house, and when fog threatens the shore, the bleating of the foghorn drifts eerily out across the lake.

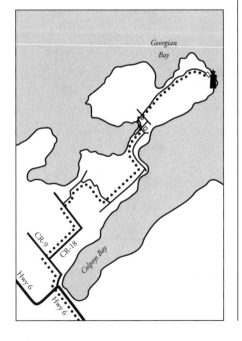

DIRECTIONS: From Wiarton take Hwy. 6 north approximately 1.8 miles (2.8 km.) to County Rd. 9. Turn right (east) onto CR-9 and go about 3.8 miles (6.1 km.), jogging north, to County Rd.18. Turn right (east) onto CR-18 and drive approximately 6.3 miles (10.1 km.) [turning sharply north at 3.3 miles (5.3 km.)] to an unnamed road to Cape Croker Park. From this point on, there are few road signs, and so we recommend taking along a good county road map as insurance.

Turn right (east) onto the unmarked road and go one mile (1.6 km.) to a Y intersection. Look for a large wooden map on the left, check your bearings if need be, and then turn onto the road headed right (south). Follow the gravel road about 2 miles (3.2 km.) to a T junction. Turn left (east) and go approximately 4.4 miles (7.1 km.), turning sharply left (north) at 2 miles (3.2 km.), bearing right (east), and again turning sharply north to a crossroad marked by a Nawash Indian Band United Church on the right. Proceed straight ahead (north) and go another 1.3 mile (2 km.) [jogging sharply right (east) at 0.8 mile (1.2 km.)] to another crossroad, this intersection marked by St. Mary's Church, on the right. Continue straight ahead on the gravel road about 4.2 miles (6.7 km.) to its end at the Cape Croker lighthouse.

CAPE CROKER LIGHTHOUSE

Lions Head Light

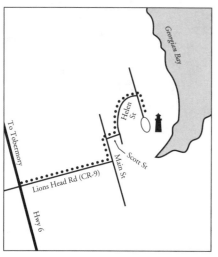

The first light here, built in 1903, was blown off its dock during a 1913 storm. The replacement light was built on a breakwater and then in 1967 moved to shore where it now rests in retirement.

The 15-foot-tall structure is typical of Canadian Range light design. The square wooden base stretches upward and narrows to a square metal railing and walkway surrounding the square wooden lantern room. The white tower is trimmed in red, and a large, black rudder on display provides a dark contrast.

A small steel light now stands at the end of the breakwater.

DIRECTIONS: From Hwy. 6 approximately 28 miles (45 km.) south of Tobermory, turn east onto County Rd. 9 (Lions Head Rd./ Ferndale Rd.) and go approximately 2 miles (3.2 km) to a stop sign at Main St. in the town of Lions Head. Turn left (north) onto Main and go 0.5 mile (0.8 km.) to Scott St. Turn right (east) onto Scott and go about one block to Helen St. Turn left (north) onto Helen and go about 0.3 mile (0.5 km.), bearing right to a T intersection. Turn right and immediately after turning look for the old range light on the left.

Cabot Head Lighthouse Museum

The two-story keeper's house at Cabot Head is a large, white clapboard-sided structure with a small addition at the rear providing even more space. Bright red trim surrounds doors, windows, and a pair of pretty dormers, but the tower was removed from the red shingled roof long ago and its whereabouts or fate is unknown.

The Friends of Cabot Head (R.R.1, Miller Lake, Ontario N0H 1Z0) are restoring the 1896 lighthouse, which they have turned into a Marine and Timber Museum. A modern front entrance deck greets visitors but inside, antiques, beautiful hardwood floors, and decorative ceilings revive an era long past. The group hopes to eventually top the building with a replica tower.

A wide expanse of unadorned lawn surrounds the building, and a fringe of bushes buffers the yard from Lake Huron. Nearby, a white steel tower, built in 1989, rises more than 40 feet to a wide platform that holds a large, automated beacon.

" Antiques, beautiful hardwood floors, and decorative ceilings revive an era long past. "

DIRECTIONS: From Hwy. 6 approximately 2 miles (3.2 km.) north of Miller Lake, turn east onto Dyer's Bay Rd. and go about 6.1 miles (9.8 km.) to the village of Dyer's Bay. Turn north, continuing on Dyer's Bay Rd. another 1.7 miles (2.7 km.) to the junction with a gravel road. Turn sharply right (east), continuing to follow blacktopped Dyer's Bay Rd., and go about 0.2 mile (0.3 km.) to the junction with a gravel road marked by a sign reading, "Wingfield Basin & Cabot Head, Travel at your own risk." Turn right (northeast) onto the gravel road and go about 5 miles (8 km.) to the parking area at the lighthouse museum. Though this is a good gravel road, it is narrow, and we recommend that you not attempt the trip in a large recreational vehicle.

After parking you must walk the last 100 yards down the road to the lighthouse.

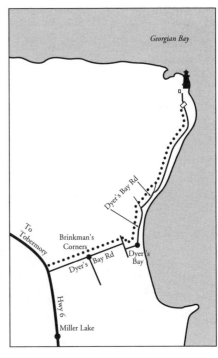

Lonely Island Lighthouse

" Ship captains faced a thick blanket of fog in the area nearly every morning."

Lonely Island is an almost perfectly round, mile-plus-wide body of land in Georgian Bay 20 miles north of the Bruce Peninsula and 10 miles southeast of Manitoulin Island. Its thickly wooded interior slopes down to a flat shoreline, and a wide section near the north shore has been cleared to accommodate the buildings of the lightstation. The shoreline guards the complex in near perfect symmetry, its brown gravel stretching in a straight line across in front. To the west where the shoreline angles sharply away, a curving cement dock stretches out into the turquoise lake. A second, smaller dock is paired with the first, creating a small slip once suitable for docking a boat. Today, a substantial section of the end of the longer dock has fallen into the water, and the other dock descends gently before submerging in the lake.

A path leads from the docks, past a helipad and a small building to the keeper's house, a white, red-roofed two-story building large enough to accommodate several people. A smaller, one-story house is joined to the first by a simple sidewalk bordered by a few large bushes. A few small bushes dot the rest of the compound, and closer to the forest's edge, larger bushes and trees are encroaching. But the gravelly soil offers little footing for lawns of any type.

Established in 1870, the light on Lonely Island is perched much farther inland, on a small plateau near the center of the island. A walkway from the dwellings cuts through the thick pine forest to a stairway providing access to the clearing around the tower. The white, octagonal tower rises to a red metal walkway and lantern room, and a curved roof with round ventilator completes the 54-foot-tall structure. Below, a helicopter pad provides much easier — though more expensive — access to the light than the arduous trail. A long, white building rests beside fuel tanks, and solar panels provide power for the isolated light.

In 1888 the French lightkeeper here wrote to the Department of Marine and Fisheries and requested a fog alarm. Ship captains — who faced a thick blanket of fog in the area nearly every morning — repeated the request for the next 14 years. But because of the island's shape and size and because ships approached from all directions, building a fog signal in one location was not feasible in the department's eyes, and it wasn't until 1944 that a suitable foghorn was finally built.

LONELY ISLAND LIGHTHOUSE (Canadian Coast Guard Photo)

Cove Island Lighthouse

"*Cove Island lighthouse is as beautiful today as the day it first illuminated the waters of Lake Huron.*"

The Cove Island lighthouse on Gig Point guards the entrance to Georgian Bay from just off the tip of the Bruce Peninsula. Another Imperial Tower, this light also warns of a dangerous submerged rock three miles to the north.

First lit in 1858, the Cove Island lighthouse is as beautiful today as the day it first illuminated the waters of Lake Huron. The circular tower is made of rough stone blocks painted a crisp white, while staggered along its sides are narrow, red-trimmed windows just large enough to afford a view of the lake. Near one of the windows on the inside, a workman scratched the date "1856" into the wet cement. At the base of the tower, a fan of bright red steps leads to an archway and door, while 80 feet above, the red lantern room rests on a stone base and is capped by a round, red metal dome. The lantern room is glazed with dozens of square panes and still displays a light that warns mariners of the dangers surrounding the island.

Just feet from the tower, the keeper's house is built of the same rough stone, and features rectangular red-trimmed windows on the first floor and a window peering out from beneath the gable at each end of the building. A one-story addition nearly touches the tower and, like the main dwelling, is roofed with beautiful red tile.

A low cement wall surrounds the structures, and a second low stone wall frames the house. Mounds of gravel rising to various heights at the beach in front of the tower attest to the fact that the waters of Lake Huron can become furious. The island's green forest frames the structures and spills down toward the water but is always held at bay by the shifting gravel.

The entire northern tip of the island is dominated by the lighthouse complex. Another residence lies east of the tower, and a 100-foot-tall, red-and-white steel radio tower stands to the west. Near the radio tower, several other buildings, including a boathouse near the rocky shore, complete the complex.

The car ferry *Chi-Cheemaun* offers a fine view of this light plus three others — Big Tub light, and the South Baymouth ranges — on its relaxing, beautiful run from Tobermory to South Baymouth. For a ferry schedule, call the Tobermory Terminal at (519) 596-2510 or the South Baymouth Terminal at (705) 859-3161.

COVE ISLAND LIGHTHOUSE

Lighthouse Point (Big Tub) Light

The first light in Tobermory was established in 1885 and was later replaced by the picturesque light still guarding the entrance to Big Tub Harbor today. Just yards from the blue waters softly lapping the rocky shoreline, the six-sided wooden tower narrows slightly as it rises and is interrupted by several rectangular windows, each bordered by red overhangs and trim. At the top of the 43-foot-tall structure, a red steel railing protects the walkway around the six-sided lantern room. The large, square panes that entirely glaze the room allow the red modern-day beacon to be seen from all directions. The tower is topped with a red metal roof and ventilator shaft and below, dark green bushes and cedars brush up against its base.

In 1985, Friends of (an underwater park named) Fathom Five, in conjunction with the St. Edmunds Township Council built a wood walkway and viewing area, making the Big Tub light more accessible to both the general public and the physically challenged.

The car ferry *Chi-Cheemaun* also offers a fine view of this light plus three others — Cove Island light, and the South Baymouth ranges — on its relaxing, beautiful run from Tobermory to South Baymouth. For a ferry schedule, call the Tobermory Terminal at (519) 596-2510 or the South Baymouth Terminal at (705) 859-3161.

Other cruises with glass-bottom boats offer fascinating, up-close looks at several nearby shipwrecks. The count of over 50 shipwrecks scattered along the lake bottom in this area are testimony of how dangerous a location Tobermory is.

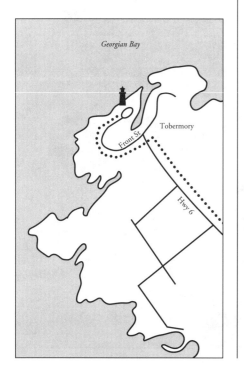

DIRECTIONS: Follow Hwy. 6 north through Tobermory to its end at the stop sign at Front St. Turn left (west) onto Front and go about 1.5 miles (2.4 km.) to its end as it turns right and then right again. From the parking area at the end of the road, walk directly toward the water about 50 feet and look for the Big Tub light, about 50 feet to the right.

To get to the ferry docks, turn right (east) onto Front St. from Hwy. 6 and go two blocks to the ticket office, on the right.

Saugeen Front and Rear Range Lights

The first light at the entrance to the Saugeen River was a front range established in 1883 by fastening a lantern to a mast on a pier.

Twenty years later a Rear Range was built on a grassy rise a quarter of a mile from the shoreline of Lake Huron, and that 32-foot-tall structure still stands today. Its wide, square base quickly narrows as it rises to a square walkway and railing surrounding the square lantern room. Entirely enclosed except for a small window at its front, the lantern room is capped in red to match the walkway and trim around the door. A wide vertical band runs up the front of the white wooden tower to assist mariners in lining up the range lights in the daytime.

This unassuming light became the center of controversy in 1989. Unannounced, the Coast Guard began peeling away its wooden siding to replace it with metal. Citizens refused to allow the defacing of their town's beloved landmark by holding an around-the-clock protective vigil for several days until the Coast Guard finally agreed to preserve the historical integrity of the guiding light.

The current Front Range light rests at the end of a narrow concrete pier stretching out 80 feet into Lake Huron and is identical to its inland sister. Electric poles run the length of the pier, their thin wires providing power for the automated light.

" The unassuming light became the center of controversy."

FRONT RANGE

REAR RANGE

🕯 DIRECTIONS: To visit the Front Range light, from Hwy. 21 (Albert St.) in Southampton turn west onto Rankin St. (the first street north of the Saugeen River) and go about 0.3 mile (0.5 km.) to where the road turns right. Look for the front range light out in front of you at this point.

To visit the Rear Range light, from Hwy. 21 turn east onto Rankin and look for the light, on the right just after turning.

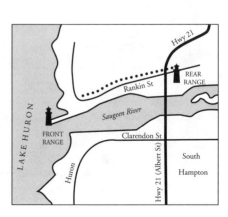

Chantry Island Lighthouse

"Entry was touchy, and several ships failed to clear the docks."

Chantry Island lighthouse, one of the Imperial Towers, is a replica of the others in nearly every way. Built in 1859, the rough stone tower rises 86 feet, its bright coat of whitewash glowing against the blue sky. At its top, a red walkway surrounds the multipaned lantern room — open to view from every angle — and the structure is capped by a domed red metal roof and ventilator ball. Emerald-green trees surround the light but are kept from reaching the water by a wide, rocky beach.

The keeper's house nearby must once have looked exactly like the one on Cove Island. But in 1954 the Chantry Island lighthouse was automated, and in the absence of a keeper, vandals took charge. The house is now a tumble-down remnant of a glorious past. Its walls are still standing, but it has lost its roof and its future doesn't look too promising.

Vandals had easy access, because the strip of water between the island and the mainland is only ¾ mile wide. At one time, in fact, manmade structures almost bridged the thin gap. One dock curved from Chantry Island out into the water. Then in 1877, what was called the "Long Dock" was completed. The structure stretched out from the mainland in a giant curve toward the first dock, leaving a gap that ships passed through to enter the harbor. Two range lights were built — one at the end of the island dock, the other on the mainland — to help ships navigate the gap.

Even so, the entry was touchy, and several ships failed to clear the docks. Finally, in 1908 the schooner *Erie Stewart* crashed into the island's dock, taking off the light tower when its mast crashed down. The light and dock were never rebuilt, to the relief of many sailors of the area, but the long dock remained into the 1930s.

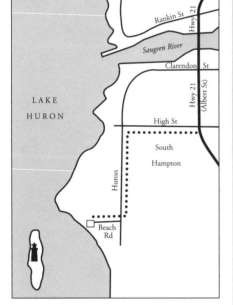

DIRECTIONS: From Hwy. 21 (Albert St.) in Southampton, turn west onto High St. and go about 0.2 mile (0.3 km.) to Huron St. Turn left (south) onto Huron and go about 0.7 mile (1.1 km.) to Beach Rd. Turn right (west) onto Beach Rd. and go about 0.3 mile (0.5 km.) to its end at Chantry Park. Look for the lighthouse about a mile out in the bay from the beach.

Kincardine Range Lighthouse Museum

"The figure of William Kay — scrupulously honest, proud, hardworking and loyal, yet still full of vinegar with a bit of the poet in him — will survive as long as his fascinating letters."

The Kincardine Rear Range lighthouse is a beautiful structure resting on the banks of the Penetangore River near where it pours into Lake Huron. The 1881 lighthouse is built into the side of a hill, and the lower level opens out to face a retaining wall that runs along the water's edge. Eight-paned windows illuminate that floor, plus the level directly above. The octagonal, white wooden tower rises up 30 feet from the house's roof, and a row of eight-paned windows facing in each direction illuminates the interior. The octagonal walkway is supported by decorative posts and protected by a metal railing. The 12-sided lantern room is only partially glazed, the rear being covered with metal siding. All the trim — from the lantern room and walkway down through the eaves, corners and windows of the house — is painted a matching bright red, giving the structure a beautiful look.

A little less than 500 yards west of the Rear Range, the small Front Range rests on a wharf extending out into the lake.

Contributing to the beauty of the Rear Range light are the efforts of William Kay, a longtime lightkeeper here. In 1885, Kay offered to not only terrace and sod the front yard with help from his family, but also, "plant a few trees, until it would look like an oasis in this desert of sand; and somewhat more becoming the fine house." In the same letter to his superiors he also asked for a fence to surround the yard, which he hoped would keep his wood from being stolen and his

"He asked for a fence, which he hoped would keep his wood from being stolen and his sheets from getting dirty from boys running under the clothesline."

sheets from getting dirty from boys running under the clothesline.

Kay wrote several such letters, and his colorful personality filled every page. The fence he asked for needed to be very strong, he said, to accept the weight of the sand on the hill behind the lighthouse. But when asked if he could build the substantial fence, he replied, "... That is impossible, and in the summer, I can't see where any light keeper could find time to build a fence, I have to sleep half the day — if it can be called a sleep when there is such a rackett on the wharf and at the fish shanties every day — and then it takes the most of the afternoon to do my cleaning and get ready for the evening, some days I have an hour or two to spare, but to go and work hard out doors would be a very bad preparation for my long watch at night, it would be different if one had an assistant to take half the night watch, but as it is, I do not see my way clear to build a fence."

A few weeks later he refused to accept a shipment of wire he had ordered, since the accompanying invoice showed a balance due of 54 cents, and he hadn't obtained departmental approval to spend any money.

In 1895, Kay reported another concern to his superiors. "I have to report, that the road from the street to the light house is all broken up by the water running from the street down on the Government property.

"I spoke to several of the councillors about it, and they blamed the chairman of the road and bridge committee a Mr. Keyworth who used to drive an old team here; but who some years ago fell heir to money in England, now he acts just as the old proverb says 'give a beggar and horse and he'll ride to the Devill.' Well he and my son quarrelled last spring when I was on a bed of sickness; about two planks Keyworth took from the lighthouse door to mend some holes in the wharf and my son was going to knock him down for it, — but excuse me — this has nothing to do with this matter.

"What should I do about the road I am placed here to look after this property, and nothing shall go wrong if I can help it. It was this same Keyworth who refused to fill up the whole with gravel at the front of the lighthouse, when the sand was all running into the basin, and the majority of the council was in favour of filling up said hole, but as Keyworth was chairman of the road and bridge committee they could not very well interfere.

"Perhaps there will be a change in the road and bridge committee next year, and I may get them to attend to this matter.

"I told them they had no right to run the water off the streets on to any ones property, and far less on to the Government property I said they ought to thank the Government for the lighthouse and take care not to injure their property.

"I am Sir your most Obedient Servant Wm Kay"

The figure of William Kay — scrupulously honest, proud, hardworking and loyal, yet still full of vinegar with a bit of the poet in him — will survive as long as his fascinating letters.

DIRECTIONS: From Hwy. 21 about midway between Goderich and Southampton, turn west onto Kincardine Ave. and go one mile (1.6 km.) to Queen St. in downtown Kincardine. Turn right (north) onto Queen and go about 0.9 mile (1.4 km.) to Harbour St. Turn left (west) onto Harbour, go about 2 blocks, then turn left (south) onto an unnamed blacktop street just before Harbour St. ends at a turnaround. Just after making the turn, you will reach the Penetangore River. The lighthouse is on the shore about 100 yards upstream.

To return to Hwy. 21, go back up Harbour St. about one block to the stop sign at Huron Terrace St. Since you cannot continue east on Harbour from this point (Harbour is one-way west), turn right (south) onto Huron Terrace and go 0.4 mile (0.6 km.) to Gordon St. Turn left (east) onto Gordon and go 0.2 mile (0.3 km.) to Queen St. Turn right (south) onto Queen and retrace the route via Kincardine Ave. back to Hwy. 21.

KINCARDINE RANGE LIGHTHOUSE

Point Clark
Lighthouse Museum

Built in 1859 as another Imperial Tower, the lighthouse at Point Clark warns of a dangerous shoal a few miles offshore. Resting just yards from the breaking Lake Huron waves, the 90-foot-high tower dominates the landscape and dwarfs the small, white keeper's house below. Only a few small, narrow windows break the circular tower's white, rough stone, and an arched doorway at the base opens to the lakeshore. Near the top, a walkway with red metal railing protects the lantern room, which is capped with a matching curved red metal roof and ventilator ball. The lantern room is entirely glazed with dozens of delicate square panes of glass, which allow you to watch clouds scuttle across the blue sky through the light as you look up from below.

In 1967, Point Clark became the first Ontario lighthouse to be declared a National Historic Site. The keeper's house has been turned into a marine museum owned by the Canadian Parks Service and operated by Huron Township. Tours are conducted regularly during museum hours, 10 a.m. to 5 p.m. from mid-June through Labor Day.

Swimming is allowed at the beach, restrooms are nearby, and benches lined up near shore invite you to refresh yourself in the cool breezes blowing across the beautiful expanse of Lake Huron.

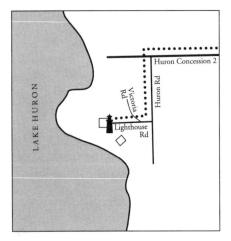

LAKE HURON

Huron Concession 2

Victoria Rd

Huron Rd

Lighthouse Rd

DIRECTIONS: From Hwy. 21 approximately 25 miles (40 km.) north of Goderich, turn west onto Huron Concession 2. The junction is marked by a sign pointing the way to "Historic Site Point Clark Lighthouse. Follow Huron Concession 2, a blacktop road, about 2.6 miles (4.2 km.) to Huron Rd. Turn left (south) onto Huron Rd. and go about 6 blocks (0.5 km) to Lighthouse Rd. Turn right (west) onto Lighthouse Rd. and go approximately 0.2 mile (0.3 km.) as it curls to the left toward the parking area at the beach and lighthouse museum, just off the road to the left.

Goderich Main Light

The Goderich Main light, built in 1847, is a heavy square tower sitting on a bluff above Lake Huron. A small room angling off one side is large enough to accommodate an entry doorway and not much else. A few rectangular windows peer out from the 35-foot-tall tower, and at the top a square walkway and railing surround the octagonal lantern room. The lantern room is entirely glazed, and you can glimpse the light from the ground. The metal cap and ventilator shaft are painted bright red, as are the walkway, railing, and trim around the door and beneath the windows.

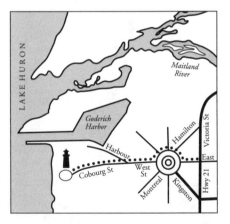

DIRECTIONS: From Hwy. 21 (Victoria St.) as you near downtown Goderich, turn west onto East St. and go one block to the town square. Turn right (north) and drive halfway around the square to West St. Turn right (west) on West St. and go 3 blocks to a Y junction. Take the left fork (Cobourg St.) 3 blocks to the turn-a-round at its end. Look for the Goderich light to the right when you reach the turn-a-round. Also look for the Goderich pierhead lights, down below the bluff and to the right in the harbor area.

ALPHABETICAL LISTING OF LIGHTHOUSES

LIGHTHOUSES YOU CAN ENTER

LIGHTHOUSES WHOSE TOWERS YOU CAN CLIMB

LIGHTHOUSE MUSEUMS

LIGHTHOUSES THAT ARE STILL ACTIVE

CHARTERS

Charter Boats

Apostle Islands Cruise Service
P.O. Box 691
Bayfield, WI 54814
(800) 323-7619 or (715) 779-3925

Choose from a variety of narrated tours to all of the Apostle Islands and area lighthouses aboard the large *Island Princess* or *Sea Queen II*. Also offered are customized trips on the smaller 27-foot Sportcraft or for a real adventure the Zodia assault craft. All personnel are well informed of the area's history. Reservations are recommended.

Brandt's Trolling Service
Captain Les Brandt
Route 1, Box 253
Washburn, WI 54891
(715) 373-5187

Lights in the area include Ashland Breakwater, La Pointe and Chequamegon Point.

Washington Island/Rock Island Ferry
Main Road
Washington Island, WI 54246
(414) 847-2252

Car and passenger ferry service to Washington Island and then passenger ferry service to Rock Island State Park to visit the Potawatomi lighthouse.

Airplanes

Aire-Dale Flying Service
Michigan City, IN 46360
Pilot — Dale J. Phillips
(219) 872-4014

Lights in the area include Michigan City, Gary Breakwall, Buffington Harbor, Indiana Harbor and Calumet Harbor.

Twin City Air Inc.
621 Bingham Ave.
Sault St. Marie, MI 49783
(906) 635-5482

Lights include Canada's Ile Parisienne, Gros Caps Reef and Caribou Island plus Michigan's Whitefish Point.

Peninsula Air, Inc.
2900 Airport
Escanaba, MI 49829
(800) 245-0888 or (906) 789-9900
Also Menominee, MI
(800) 369-0888 or (906) 863-9171

Wisconsin lights in the area include Pilot Island, Plum Island, Sherwood Point, Chambers Island, Peshtigo Reef and Long Tail Point. Michigan lights in the area (see *A Traveler's Guide to 116 Michigan Lighthouses*) include Minneapolis Shoal, Poverty Island and St. Martins Island.

Foster Aviation
Sky Harbor Airport
Duluth, MN 55802
(218) 722-6410

Lights include Superior Entry (Wisconsin Point), Minnesota Point, Two Harbors and Split Rock.

CANADA

Charter Boats

Rossport Island Tours
In season: Rossport, Ontario P0T 2R0
(800) 876-2296 or (807) 824-2887
Off season: RR16, Onion Lake Rd.
Thunder Bay, Ontario P7B 6B3
(807) 767-3006

Unique boat-and-breakfast and evening cruises. Also many day and overnight cruises to lighthouse destinations on the north shore of Lake Superior including Thunder Bay, Battle Island and the Slate Islands. Hosts are Captain Greg Richard and his wife, Lynda.

Georgian Bay Charters
Captain Darcy Noble
Charles St.
Killarney, Ontario P0M 2A0
(705) 287-2709

Water taxi service and completely outfitted fishing trips in the Killarney area. Lights include Killarney East and Killarney Northwest.

The Little Britt Inn
Britt, Ontario P0G 1A0
Captain Jerry Marcil
(705) 383-0028

Fishing and sightseeing charters. Lights in the area include Byng Inlet Range, Gereaux Island, Bustard Rocks and French River Range.

Airplanes

Thunder Bay Flying Club
417 John Patterson Dr.
Thunder Bay Airport
Thunder Bay, Ontario P7E 6M8
(807) 577-1118

Lights include Thunder Bay area, Slate Islands, Battle Island, Trowbridge Island, Point Porphyry and Shaganash.

Watson's Skyways
11 Mission Rd.
Wawa, Ontario P0S 1K0
(705) 856-4233

Fly-in fishing and scenic trips. Lights in the area include Otter Island, Davieaux Island and Michipicoten Island.

Batchawana Bay Air Services
P.O. Box 129
Batchawana Bay, Ontario P0S 1A0
Winter address: 17 Carlbert St.
Sault Ste. Marie, Ontario P8A 5R7
(705) 882-2361

Area lights include Michipicoten Island, Caribou Island, Corbeil Point and Batchawana Bay area.

Seguin Airways
Georgian Bay Airport
Parry Sound, Ontario
(705) 378-5174 or (705) 746-4956

Lights in the area include Red Rock, Snug Harbour, Western Islands, Brebeuf Range and Hope Island.

Bruce Land Air
Wiarton, Ontario N0H 2T0
(519) 534-3737

Area lights include Bruce Peninsula lights, Griffith Island, Chantry Island and Nottawasaga Island.

FERRIES

Two Great Lakes car/passenger ferries warrant special attention, as both can save miles of driving while offering splendid from-the-water views of several lights.

The S.S. *Badger*, the Great Lakes' only passenger steamship, carries passengers and vehicles on four-hour crossings of Lake Michigan between Ludington, Michigan, and Manitowoc, Wisconsin. From the decks of the 410-foot-long craft you get excellent views of the Ludington North Pierhead light and the Manitowoc North Breakwater light. For further information contact Lake Michigan Carferry, P.O. Box 708, Ludington, Michigan; (800) 841-4243, (616) 845-555 or (414) 684-0888.

The M.S. *Chi-Cheemaun* (Ojibway for "Big Canoe") makes two-hour trips between Tobermory, at the tip of Ontario's Bruce Peninsula, and South Baymouth on Manitoulin Island. This alternative to the long drive around the east shore of Georgian Bay takes you past Big Tub light, picture-perfect Cove Island lighthouse, and the South Baymouth harbor range lights. For further information call the Tobermory terminal at (519) 596-2510 or the South Baymouth terminal at (705) 859-3161.

Badger

Chi-Cheemaun

BIBLIOGRAPHY

Apostle Islands. National Park Handbook #141, U.S. Government Publication.

Campbell, William A. *Northeastern Georgian Bay and its People.* Sudbury, Ontario: Journal Printing.

Davenport, Don. "The Last Manned Lighthouse." *The Compass,* #2, 1984.

Gateman, Laura M. *Lighthouses Around Bruce County.* Chesley, Ontario: Spinning Wheel Publishing, 1991.

Krerowicz, John. "Lighthouse Top Back in Place." *Kenosha News,* May 8, 1994.

"Lonely Watches Over In Lighthouse." *The Cleveland Plain Dealer,* September 18, 1983.

"Never Reaches Apostles Light." *Duluth News-Tribune,* August 6, 1978.

Nuhfer, Edward B., and Mary P. Dalles. *A Guidebook to the Geology of Lake Superior's Apostle Islands National Lakeshore.* Dubuque, Iowa: W.C. Brown Publishers, 1987.

Pearen, Shelley J. *Exploring Manitoulin.* Toronto: University of Toronto Press, 1992.

Poyner, Heather Larson, "Lighthouse Goes to High Places." *Kenosha News,* September 12, 1994.

Sandell, Marion E. *Keepers of the Light: Nottawasaga Island 1858-1983.* Collingwood, Ontario: The Print Shop Collingwood Limited, 1993.

Special Collections, Canadian National Archives, Ottawa, Ontario.

Special Collections, Sault Sainte Marie Public Library, Sault Sainte Marie, Ontario.

Special Collections, Great Lakes Lighthouse Society Reference Library, Vermilion, Ohio.

Strzok, Dave. *A Visitor's Guide to the Apostle Islands National Lakeshore.* Ashland, Wisconsin: Superior Printing and Specialities, 1981.

Weeks-Mifflin, Mary, and Ray Mifflin. *The Light on Chantry Island.* Erin, Ontario: Boston Mills Press, 1986.

THE AUTHORS

The Penrose family resides in rural West Branch, Michigan. Bill, 55, has worked for the Pepsi Cola Company for 29 years. He enjoys exploring and photographing the Great Lakes with his wife, Ruth, 54, who works full time as an X-ray technician in their home area.

Their daughter Laurie, 32, in addition to writing devotes time to her and husband Ross' two children, Masina, 6, and Alex, 3. Bill Penrose Jr., 26, is hard at work transforming the thousands of Michigan outdoor photographs the Penroses have taken over the years into a viable family business.

This is the Penroses' fourth family-effort book. *A Guide to 199 Michigan Waterfalls* was published in 1988, *A Traveler's Guide to 116 Michigan Lighthouses* was published in 1992, and *A Traveler's Guide to 100 Eastern Great Lakes Lighthouses* was published in 1994.